creating a
photo book and slideshow
with iPhoto 5

Visual QuickProject Guide

by Elizabeth Castro

**Peachpit
Press**

Visual QuickProject Guide
Creating a Photo Book and Slideshow with iPhoto 5
Elizabeth Castro

Peachpit Press
1249 Eighth Street
Berkeley, CA 94710
510/524-2178
800/283-9444
510/524-2221 (fax)

Find us on the World Wide Web at: www.peachpit.com
To report errors, please send a note to errata@peachpit.com
Peachpit Press is a division of Pearson Education

Cover design: The Visual Group with Aren Howell
Cover photo credit: Elizabeth Castro
Interior design: Elizabeth Castro

ISBN 0-321-35752-3

9 8 7 6 5 4 3 2 1
Printed and bound in the United States of America

For Andreu - my partner, my witness, my love

Every photographer dips her camera in her own soul,
and paints her own nature into her photographs.

adapted from Henry Ward Beecher,
U.S. abolitionist & clergyman (1813–1887)

Special thanks to...

Lupe Edgar at Peachpit Press, who helped shepherd this
book through production, and

Nancy Davis, my wonderful editor at Peachpit Press, to
whom I owe so much. (Same as last time, but still
heartfelt, still so true.)

contents

introduction   vii

what you'll do	viii	the web site	xiii
how this book works	x	the next step	xiv

1. importing and organizing photos   1

get photos from camera	2	organize with albums	12
get photos from a disk	3	drag new albums	14
view and sort film rolls	4	organize with folders	15
increase viewing size	5	define keywords	16
rotate photos	6	apply keywords	18
review your photos	7	search by keywords	19
get rid of the bad ones	8	search by date	20
empty the trash	9	search by text	21
label your photos	10	sort your photos	22
rate your photos	11	extra bits	23

2. creating a photo book   31

choose photos for book	32	change page design	50
put photos in order	34	rearrange photos	52
choose a book theme	36	create a panorama	54
use the book mode	38	drag to change design	56
organize the book files	39	control overlapping	58
place photos on cover	40	remove photos	59
magnify the view	42	autoflow the photos	60
edit text	43	add photos to book	62
navigate to next page	44	finish placing photos	63
change the page type	45	reorder pages	64
fix red eye	46	remove pages	65
enlarge and center	48	order book	66
view a two-page spread	49	extra bits	68

contents

3. making a slideshow   73

import photos	74	pan from one half...	90
put photos in order	75	...to the other half	91
create a slideshow	76	add and reorder photos	92
adjust default settings	78	add new transition	93
crop photos	80	auto enhance photos	94
duplicate a photo	82	custom adjust photos	95
display in black/white	83	change wipe direction	96
adjust transition	84	add music	98
zoom in and center	85	play a slideshow	100
add motion to slides	86	share a slideshow	101
crop a photo into two	88	extra bits	102

appendix a: photo book themes   107

picture book	108	classic	126
travel	114	story book	128
watercolor	116	collage	130
contemporary	118	portfolio	132
folio	120	year book	134
crayon	122	catalog	136
baby boy or girl	124	extra bits	138

index   141

introduction

The Visual QuickProject Guide that you hold in your hands offers a unique way to learn about new technologies. Instead of drowning you in theoretical possibilities and lengthy explanations, this Visual QuickProject Guide uses big, color illustrations coupled with clear, concise step-by-step instructions to show you how to complete two specific projects in a matter of hours.

Our projects in this book are to create a photo book and a slideshow from a library of digital photos using Apple's iPhoto software. iPhoto is an ingenious program that first helps you organize your photos with its labels and keywords, and then offers beautiful layouts for displaying your photos on paper or on screen. The photo book and slideshow that you'll create in this book chronicle the adventures of a trip to Barcelona. Because the projects cover all the basic techniques, you'll be able to use what you learn to create all sorts of other photo books and slideshows—perhaps to share pictures of your children with relatives, make a family heirloom album of photographs from your brother's wedding, develop a product catalog for your business, or create an onscreen portfolio of your artwork.

Why use iPhoto to organize your photos and create photo books and slideshows? Digital cameras free you to take thousands of photos. Too bad they're all labeled something like "4653.jpg". iPhoto helps you organize your photos so you can find them, and then provides intuitive, powerful tools for combining them into beautiful collections that you can view on paper or on screen.

what you'll do

Create albums for similarly
themed photographs and
organize them in labeled folders.

Organize imported photos into
labeled and dated film rolls.

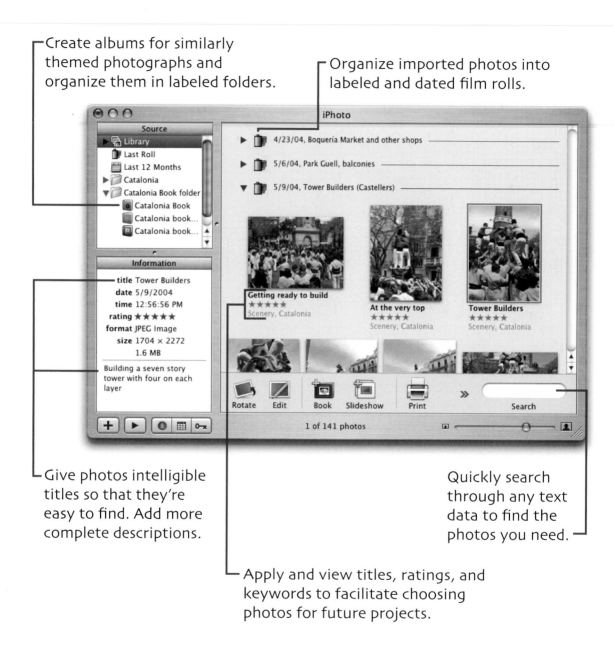

Give photos intelligible
titles so that they're
easy to find. Add more
complete descriptions.

Quickly search
through any text
data to find the
photos you need.

Apply and view titles, ratings, and
keywords to facilitate choosing
photos for future projects.

In the first project, you'll make a beautiful, professionally printed and bound photo book that chronicles a trip to Barcelona.

In the second project, you'll create a digital slideshow with custom transitions that you can later show on your computer monitor, television, or digital projector.

how this book works

The title of each section explains what is covered on that page or spread.

Captions explain how to follow each procedure, and what happens when you do.

Important concepts and iPhoto command names and tools are displayed in orange.

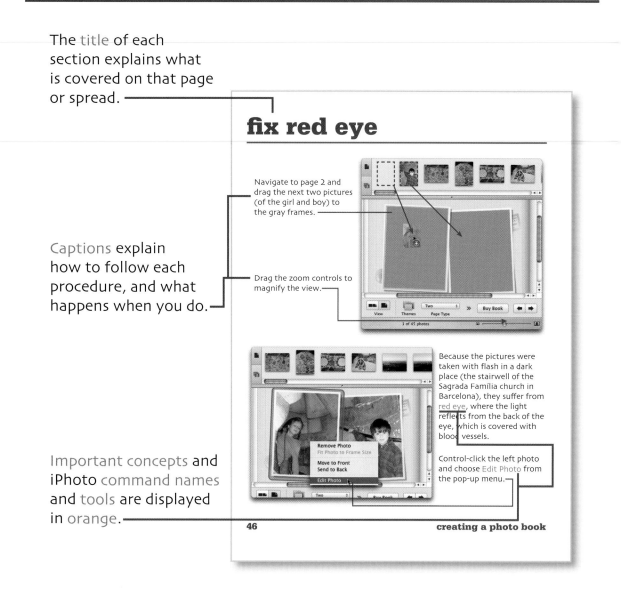

fix red eye

Navigate to page 2 and drag the next two pictures (of the girl and boy) to the gray frames.

Drag the zoom controls to magnify the view.

Because the pictures were taken with flash in a dark place (the stairwell of the Sagrada Família church in Barcelona), they suffer from red eye, where the light reflects from the back of the eye, which is covered with blood vessels.

Control-click the left photo and choose Edit Photo from the pop-up menu.

46   **creating a photo book**

               introduction

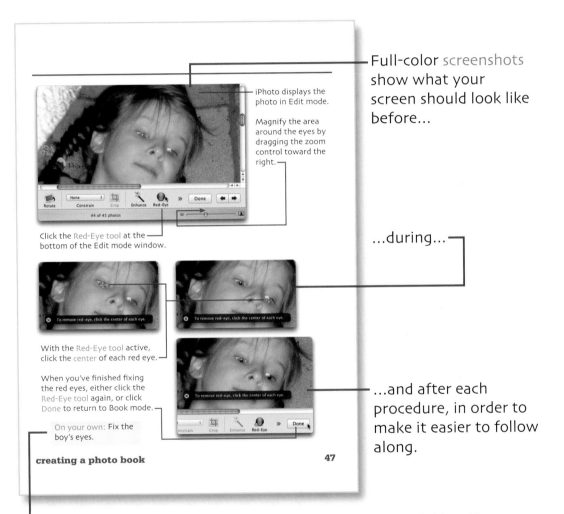

Full-color screenshots show what your screen should look like before...

iPhoto displays the photo in Edit mode.

Magnify the area around the eyes by dragging the zoom control toward the right.

Click the Red-Eye tool at the bottom of the Edit mode window.

...during...

With the Red-Eye tool active, click the center of each red eye.

When you've finished fixing the red eyes, either click the Red-Eye tool again, or click Done to return to Book mode.

On your own: Fix the boy's eyes.

...and after each procedure, in order to make it easier to follow along.

creating a photo book   47

The On your own areas, with an orange background, identify the few steps of the project that are not shown in this book (since they are identical to a procedure that you've just completed). You can repeat these techniques for practice, or so that you can finish the project exactly as I have.

introduction   **xi**

how this book works

The extra bits section at the end of each chapter contains additional tips and tricks that you might like to know—but that aren't absolutely necessary for creating the project.

The heading for each group of tips matches the section title. (The colors are just for separating one section's tips from the next and have no other hidden meaning.)

zoom in and center

extra bits

display in black/white p. 83
- The black and white effect only applies to the photo in this slideshow. The photo will continue to be shown normally in the other slideshows or books that contain it, as well as in the main window.
- You can also create a sepia effect (a sort of old-fashioned, yellowed look) by choosing Sepia instead of Black and White in the Effect menu. Again, it only affects the slide in the current slideshow, not in other slideshows or books.

adjust transition p. 84
- We set the default duration, transition, and transition speed back on page 78. These will apply to all slides until and unless you change them as described here.
- You can select more than one photo at a time (in the slideshow's photo browser) and apply a new duration, transition, or transition speed to all of them at once.
- You can also get to the Adjust This Slide box by clicking the Adjust button at the bottom of the Slideshow window or, if the button is not visible, by choosing it from the >> menu at the bottom of the Slideshow window.

- You can leave the Adjust This Slide box open all the time, if you wish. Changes are applied as you make them and thus you don't have to close the box to apply the changes or to start working on other slides.

zoom in and center p. 85
- Zooming in on a photo, in contrast with cropping, does not affect it in any other slideshow or book.

add motion to slides p. 86
- The Start/End toggle simply shows you whether you're looking at the initial or the final position and zoom for the photo. So, if you want to see the initial position and zoom, click the Start/End toggle until Start is selected. If you want to change the initial position and zoom, click the Start/End toggle until Start is selected and then adjust the position and zoom. In the same way, if you want to see the final position, click the Start/End toggle until End is selected. If you want to change the final position and zoom, click the Start/End toggle until End is selected and then adjust the position and zoom.

104   making a slideshow

Next to the heading there's a page number that also shows which section the tips belong to.

the web site

You can find this book's companion web site
at http://www.cookwood.com/iphotovqj/

```
●●●  Creating a Photo Book and Slideshow with iPhoto, Visual QuickProject Guide – Examples
◄▾  ▶▾  ⟳  ⊗  ⌂  www.cookwood.com/iphotovqj/examples/          ▾  ▶  Gᐧ
Brass in Pocket   BlogThis!   Fiber resources ▾   homeschool ▾   iPhoto ▾   1:24 PM   Genealogy ▾
```

creating a photo book and slideshow with iphoto: vqj

about | examples | extras | errata | opinions | home

examples
about
download

These Web pages contain all the images used to create the projects in the book Creating a Photo Book and Slideshow with iPhoto: Visual QuickProject Guide written by Elizabeth Castro. You may download the images and use them to follow along with the projects in the book, but you may not otherwise publish them (in print or electronically), create derivative works from them, or distribute the original or derivative works to others. By downloading the images, you agree to these terms. If you are interested in using the photos for some other purpose, please contact me first.

Because the images are so large, they take a long time to download. I have provided both full-size and reduced-size collections so that readers with slower internet connections can also use the images. Note, however, that when creating the book project, the smaller images may generate yellow warning triangles since they don't have a high enough resolution for printing.

The images of the Pedrera were used in this book with the kind permission of Fundació Caixa Catalunya (though they belong to me and were taken by me). They asked that I only provide low-resolution versions with the book, so I'm afraid that's all you'll find here.

I have also provided a QuickTime movie of the slideshow project so that you can see what it looks like when it's finished.

I must also note that I'm providing these images in good faith. If I find that letting people download them is taking up too much bandwidth, I may have to restrict them further, or only provide the low resolution versions. I'd like not to have to do that, because I think it's helpful to have real images to play with. You can help me by not downloading them more than once (wherever possible) and by using them in accordance with the terms outlined above. Thanks.

Photo Book
High Resolution photos
Low Resolution photos

Slideshow
High Resolution photos
Low Resolution photos
Slideshow QuickTime Movie

```
Done
```

You'll find the image files for both the photo book and the slideshow projects, as well as a QuickTime movie of the final slideshow so that you can see how it looks when it's finished.

the next step

While this Visual QuickProject Guide will you give you an excellent foundation in iPhoto, it focuses heavily on importing and organizing photos, creating photo books, and making slideshows. But iPhoto can also help you create Web pages, order prints of your photos, and print copies on your own printer, among other things. For a full reference guide, you might consider Adam Engst's excellent iPhoto 5 for Mac OS X: Visual QuickStart Guide, also published by Peachpit Press.

Over 400 Tips and Techniques!

VISUAL QUICKSTART GUIDE

ADAM C. ENGST

iPHOTO
FOR MAC OS X

5

Teach yourself iPhoto the quick and easy way! This Visual QuickStart Guide uses pictures rather than lengthy ...anations. You'll be up ...running in no time!

Editing Photos

Cropping Photos

If you are planning to print a photo or display it on your Desktop, you should crop it using an appropriate aspect ratio. (See "Understanding Aspect Ratios" in Appendix A, "Deep Background," for details.) Even if you don't plan to print a photo, cropping extraneous detail can improve an image.

To crop a photo:

1. Select the desired portion of the image, using a constrain setting if you plan to use the image for display or printing.

2. Click the Crop button in the edit pane or the image-editing window's toolbar, or (Control)-click and choose Crop from the contextual menu.
   iPhoto deletes the fogged area of the picture, leaving just what you had selected (**Figure 4.18** and **Figure 4.19**).

✔ Tips

■ Pressing and releasing (Control) no longer toggles between the "before" and "after" views when you're cropping in iPhoto 5.

■ If your selection rectangle is very close to one of the standard aspect ratios, it's best to use the standard aspect ratio in case you want to print the image later.

■ When you crop a photo, you remove pixels from it. So if you crop a 1600 x 1200 pixel photo (1,920,000 pixels) down to 1200 x 900 (1,080,000 pixels), you've removed almost half the image. Thus, if you print the original and the cropped version at the same size, the original will be of a much higher quality. Heavy cropping is one reason why iPhoto shows a low-resolution warning icon when you're creating books or prints. For details, see "Understanding Resolution" in Appendix A, "Deep Background."

Figure 4.18 To crop an image, select the desired portion and then click the Crop button. Here I've cropped out all the irrelevant background around the insect.

Figure 4.19 As you can see, cropping this image improves it immensely.

Adjust Shooting Style

When taking pictures, you usually want to fill the frame with the scene, but if you plan to order prints of all your photos, you might want to include a little extra space on the edges to allow for cropping to a print aspect ratio. See Appendix B, "Taking Better Photos," for more tips!

CROPPING PHOTOS

69

The iPhoto VQS features clear examples, concise, step-by-step instructions, hundreds of illustrations, and lots of helpful tips. It covers every aspect of iPhoto in detail.

1. importing and organizing photos

The first week you get a digital camera, you experience the freedom of taking dozens of pictures, in the hope that you capture the perfect shot. The second week, with hundreds of pictures under your belt, you begin to worry how you're going to find those pictures of your son's birthday party. The third week you're saved: you find iPhoto.

iPhoto is an excellent digital photo organizer. In this chapter, you'll learn how to bring photos into iPhoto from your digital camera, from your email, and from the folders on your computer (where you may have stored digital images that you scanned in from printed photographs).

Next, you'll learn how to label your photos, add descriptions, mark them with keywords, and give them ratings. iPhoto then offers powerful tools for searching through both the information you've added as well as the date information that was provided by your camera.

iPhoto helps you locate the photos you want, when you want them.

get photos from camera

Connect your camera to your Mac, and turn it on. iPhoto will launch automatically and show the camera in the Source list.

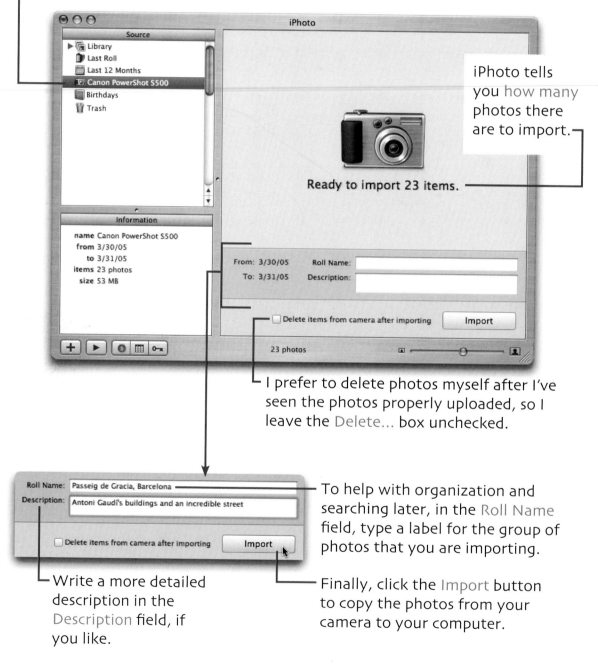

iPhoto tells you how many photos there are to import.

I prefer to delete photos myself after I've seen the photos properly uploaded, so I leave the Delete... box unchecked.

To help with organization and searching later, in the Roll Name field, type a label for the group of photos that you are importing.

Write a more detailed description in the Description field, if you like.

Finally, click the Import button to copy the photos from your camera to your computer.

get photos from a disk

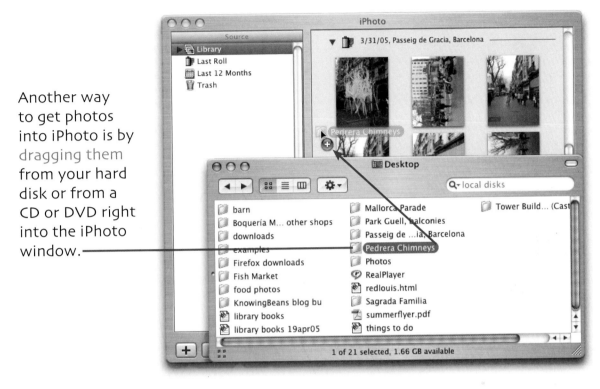

Another way to get photos into iPhoto is by dragging them from your hard disk or from a CD or DVD right into the iPhoto window.

Each time you import photos, iPhoto places them in your Library in a new film roll. The film roll gets its name from the Roll Name field if you import from a camera (see previous page) or from the folder name if you drag from a folder on your Mac.

view and sort film rolls

Make sure Film Rolls is checked in the View menu so that you can see your Library divided into groups of photos that were imported at the same time.

Choose View > Sort Photos > by Film Roll to organize the photos in your Library according to the film rolls to which they belong.

Make sure Library is selected in the Source list.

Each film roll is identified by its name and ordered by the date it was created.

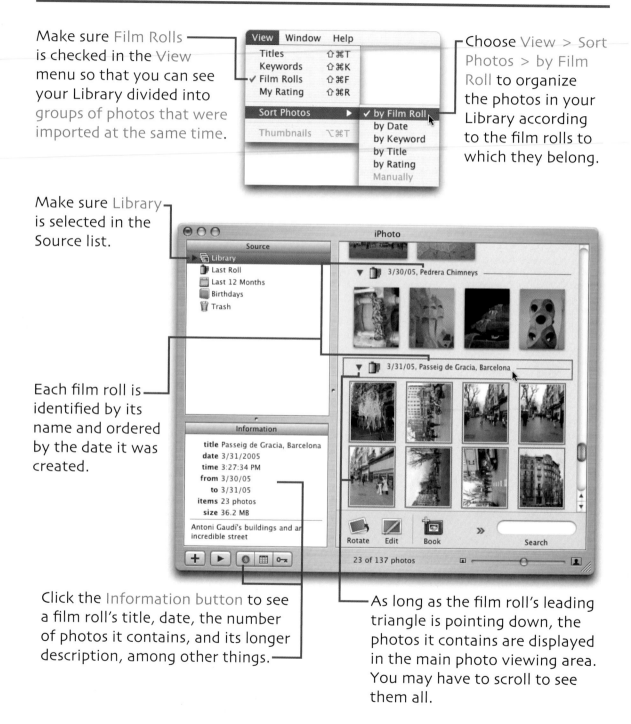

Click the Information button to see a film roll's title, date, the number of photos it contains, and its longer description, among other things.

As long as the film roll's leading triangle is pointing down, the photos it contains are displayed in the main photo viewing area. You may have to scroll to see them all.

increase viewing size

You can view the photos in the viewing area at practically any size. Sometimes, to pick out the photo you want, it's more helpful to see a whole bunch of them on the screen at once. In this case, you'd want them smaller.

But if you need to see each individual one more clearly, drag the blue ball on the size control toward the right to make them larger...instantly!

importing and organizing photos

rotate photos

If some of your photos are oriented the wrong way, simply select them and click the Rotate button at the bottom of the iPhoto window. (Option-click the Rotate button to spin them in the opposite direction.)

The landscape-oriented photos are now properly displayed.

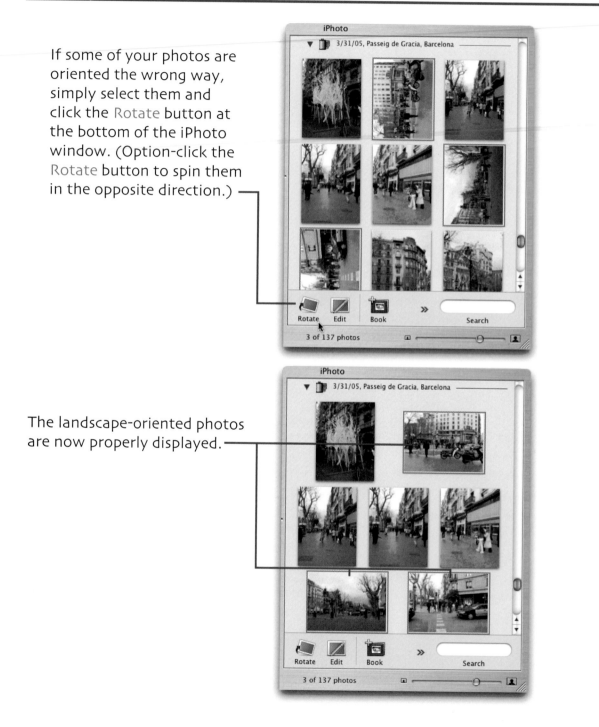

importing and organizing photos

review your photos

Once you've imported your photos, you want to take a good look at them with your monitor—which, no matter how small, is always larger than a digital camera's LCD screen. Start by clicking the film roll label in the main viewing area.

Then click the Play button down in the lower-left corner of iPhoto's window.

For a simple review, put the speed of the transition to its maximum value so that you can see more photo and less transition.

Play each slide for 3 seconds (or less) and uncheck all the remaining options. This way you can concentrate on content, not the style of the slideshow (which we'll get to in Chapter 3).

Click Play to start the review.

get rid of the bad ones

Digital cameras free you to take as many shots as you want. Inevitably some of them will be blurry or just plain bad. To remove a photo from your Library, select it...

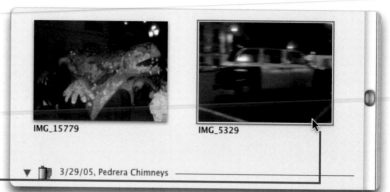

IMG_15779 IMG_5329

3/29/05, Pedrera Chimneys

...and choose Move to Trash in the Photos menu.

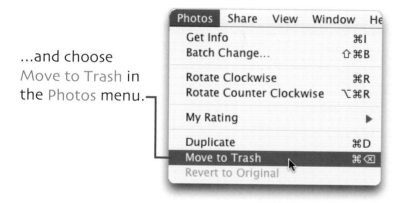

Photos Share View Window He

Get Info   ⌘I
Batch Change...   ⇧⌘B

Rotate Clockwise   ⌘R
Rotate Counter Clockwise ⌥⌘R

My Rating   ▶

Duplicate   ⌘D
Move to Trash   ⌘⌫
Revert to Original

The photo is removed from the Library.

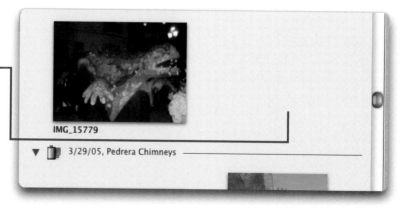

IMG_15779

3/29/05, Pedrera Chimneys

importing and organizing photos

empty the trash

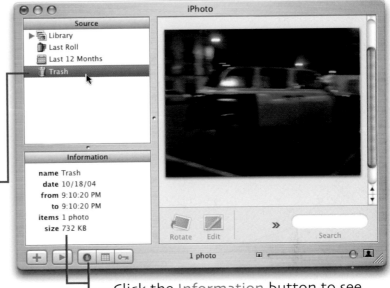

When you delete a photo from the Library, it doesn't disappear completely; it's placed in the Trash. You can see all the photos in the Trash by clicking the Trash icon in the Source list.

Click the Information button to see more details about what's in the Trash.

You then have two choices. To remove the photo completely (with no possibility of getting it back), choose iPhoto > Empty Trash.

To take it out of the Trash and put it back in your Library, choose Photos > Restore to Photo Library.

label your photos

While labeling film rolls as we did on page 2 is a good start, labeling individual photos makes finding them later very easy. Select the photo that you want to label.

Click the Information button at the bottom-left corner of the iPhoto window.

Information

title	IMG_9887
date	3/30/2005
time	1:25:29 PM
rating	· · · · ·
format	JPEG Image
size	1704 × 2272
	1.7 MB
comments	

The title, by default, is the file name of the photo.

Information

title	White fountain
date	3/30/2005
time	1:25:29 PM
rating	· · · · ·
format	JPEG Image
size	1704 × 2272
	1.7 MB

The kids loved these streams of paper blowing up from the vent.

Replace the default title with a more descriptive title. Add comments, if you like.

View	Window	Help
Titles		⇧⌘T
Keywords		⇧⌘K
✓ Film Rolls		⇧⌘F
My Rating		⇧⌘R
Sort Photos		▶
Thumbnails		⌥⌘T

Then when you choose View > Titles...

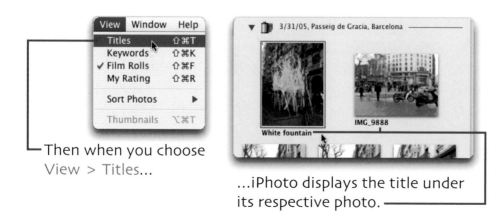

...iPhoto displays the title under its respective photo.

rate your photos

A rating is a good way to identify the best photos in your collection so that you can easily find them later when you're ready to make a slideshow or photo book. To begin, select a photo.

Choose Photos > My Rating and decide how many stars to give each photo.

To see the ratings next to your photos in the main viewing area, choose View > My Rating.

The rating is displayed below the corresponding photo.

organize with albums

An album is a group of related pictures that will generally be used to create something: perhaps prints, a web page, or as you'll see later in this book, a photo book or slideshow. Create a new album by choosing File > New Album.

File	Edit	Photos	Share	View	Win
New Album...					⌘N
New Book					
New Slideshow					
New Album From Selection...					⇧⌘N
New Smart Album...					⌥⌘N
New Folder					
Create Film Roll					
Add to Library...					⌘O
Close Window					⌘W
Edit Smart Album					
Page Setup...					⇧⌘P
Print...					⌘P

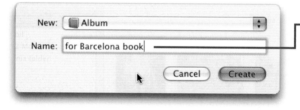

Give the new album a name, either to denote what it contains or what it will be used for. Then click Create.

The new album is listed at the end of the Source list at the left side of the iPhoto window. Albums have a little blue album icon.

Drag photos to the album from different film rolls (or other albums).

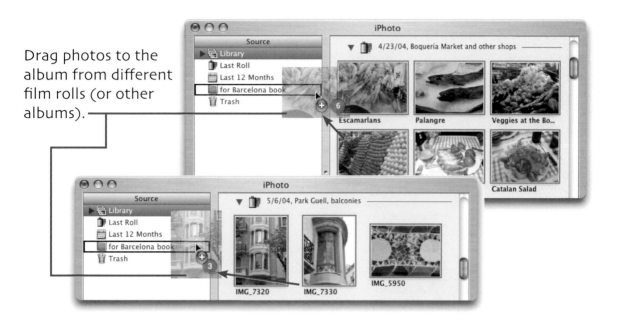

When you select the album, you can see the photos that it contains.

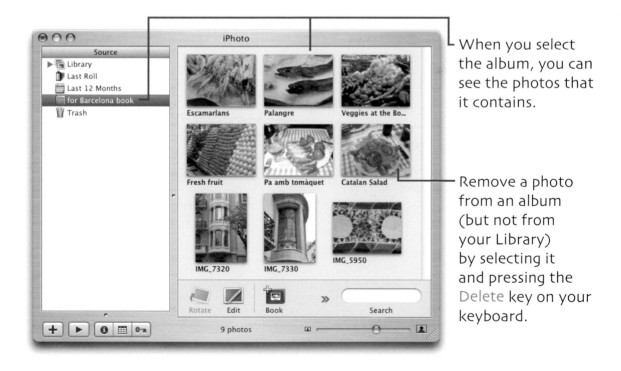

Remove a photo from an album (but not from your Library) by selecting it and pressing the Delete key on your keyboard.

drag new albums

You can also drag photos to an empty space in the Source list to create a new album for the selected photos.

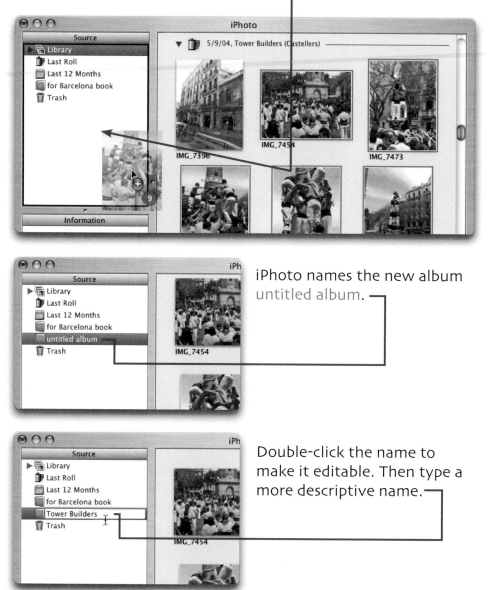

iPhoto names the new album untitled album.

Double-click the name to make it editable. Then type a more descriptive name.

importing and organizing photos

organize with folders

A folder is a good way to organize similar albums, together with the projects that you create out of them, like photo books and slideshows. To create one, choose File > New Folder.

All folders are listed at the top of your window, under the Library and its subsets (Last Roll and Last 12 Months). Type a name for your new folder.

Drag the for Barcelona book and Tower Builders albums into the new Catalonia folder until it is outlined in black.

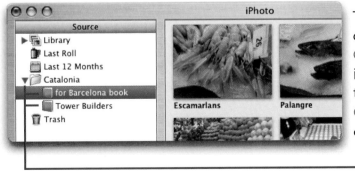

The albums are now displayed below the Catalonia folder, slightly indented. Click the triangle to the left of Catalonia to hide its contents.

define keywords

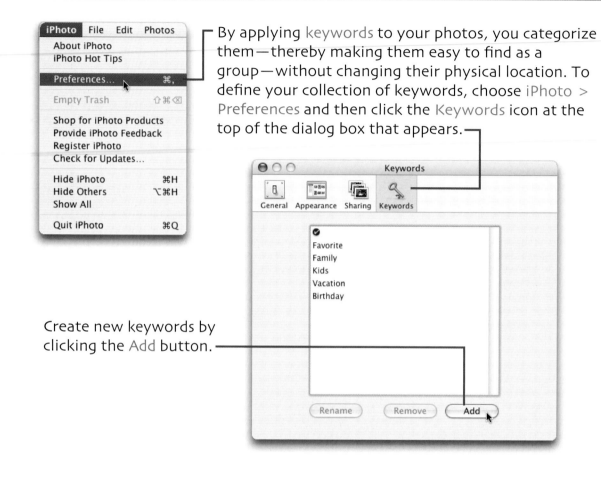

By applying keywords to your photos, you categorize them—thereby making them easy to find as a group—without changing their physical location. To define your collection of keywords, choose iPhoto > Preferences and then click the Keywords icon at the top of the dialog box that appears.

Create new keywords by clicking the Add button.

A new untitled keyword is created.

Type the new keyword name.

On your own: Create a keyword for Scenery as well.

I find iPhoto's default keywords less than useful for my subject matter. If you agree, you can make them better by selecting the Keyword name, clicking the Rename button and typing a new name.

You can also simply delete any keywords you have no use for. Select the offending keyword and click Remove.

Keywords are listed in the order in which they were created.

apply keywords

To add a keyword to one or more photos, drag the photos onto the desired keyword in the Keywords list until the keyword is framed in blue.

If you can't see the Keywords list, click the blue key to make it appear.

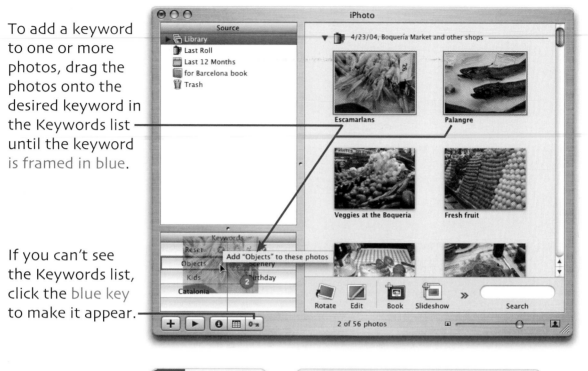

To view the applied keywords under the photos in the photo viewing area, choose View > Keywords.

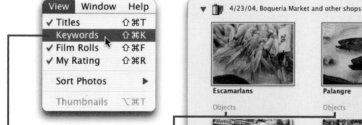

On your own: Apply the Catalonia keyword to all the photos for this project.

search by keywords

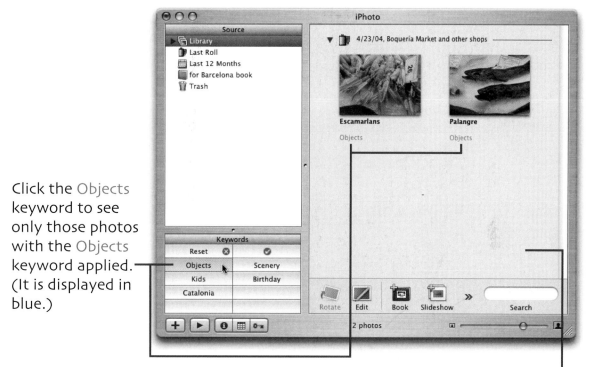

Click the Objects keyword to see only those photos with the Objects keyword applied. (It is displayed in blue.)

The photos that do not have the Objects keyword applied disappear from view.

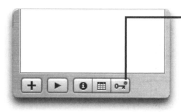

If you close the keyword list while you're searching by keywords (by clicking the blue key at the bottom left of the iPhoto window), a small blue dot indicates that the search is active. (That's where all those photos went!)

search by date

Click the little calendar icon in the bottom-left corner of the iPhoto window to reveal the calendar search tool.

The boldface titles indicate the time periods for which you have photos. Hover over one to see how many photos are dated within that period.

Click the forward arrow or double-click the month name to see the individual days of the month. (Click the backward arrow to move out again.)

Click the up and down arrows to see the preceding or following time period (in this case, 2003 or 2005).

Click a year, month, or day to view only the photos that are dated accordingly. The dates will be shown in blue. Shift-click to add consecutive days or months. Command-click to add non-consecutive days or months. And Option-click to choose a particular day or month in all years.

Click the circled x to cancel the calendar search and to view all photos regardless of their date.

When the calendar is hidden, a blue dot on the calendar icon indicates an active search by date.

search by text

Type a few letters into the Search box in the lower-right corner of iPhoto's window to quickly find the corresponding photo. The search box looks at titles, comments, film roll names, file names, and keywords.

Click the circled x to cancel the search by text.

sort your photos

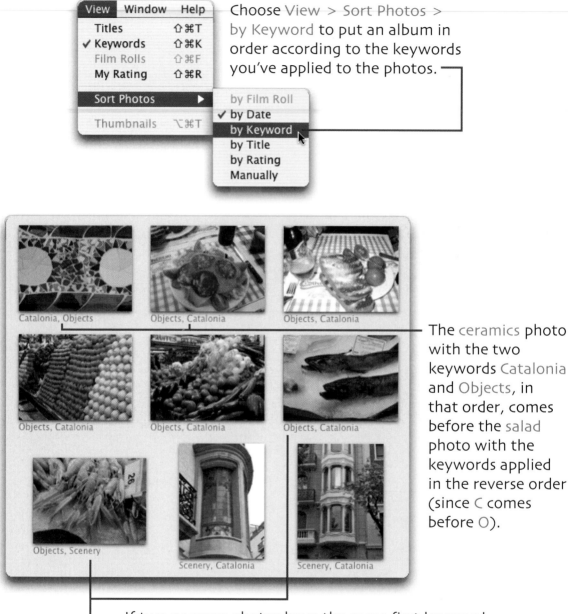

Choose View > Sort Photos > by Keyword to put an album in order according to the keywords you've applied to the photos.

The ceramics photo with the two keywords Catalonia and Objects, in that order, comes before the salad photo with the keywords applied in the reverse order (since C comes before O).

If two or more photos have the same first keyword, they are sorted according to the second keyword. (And so on.)

importing and organizing photos

extra bits

get photos from camera p. 2

- iPhoto should open automatically when you plug your camera into your Mac. If it doesn't, open the Image Capture program (really!) that is in your Applications folder and choose Preferences. Then, in the Camera pane, select iPhoto next to When a camera is connected, open:.

- Some cameras have to be in Play mode in order to trigger iPhoto to open.

- Some cameras need to be dismounted before they can be disconnected. Click the eject icon next to their name in the Source list in order to dismount them.

- Once you disconnect your camera from your computer, it will disappear from the Source list.

get photos from a disk p. 3

- You can download the photos used to create the projects in this book from the web site (see page xiii). Then drag them to iPhoto as described here.

- You don't have to drag a whole folder. You can drag individual images into iPhoto from the Finder.

- You can also drag photos to iPhoto from an email. This is a quick and easy way to add the pictures that your sister sent you of your niece into your iPhoto library.

- If you drag a folder to the main part of the iPhoto window, you'll get a new film roll with the same name as the folder, as shown. If you drag a folder to the Source list at the left of the iPhoto window, you'll get a new album as well as a new film roll with the same name as the folder. For more details, see page 14.

- Dragging photos into iPhoto is also the easiest way to get scanned photos into your library.

- You can also choose File > Add to Library and choose the folder that contains the photographs you wish to import.

view and sort film rolls p. 4

- Film rolls are designed to identify groups of photos that were imported together (and thus may have something to do with each other). However, the current version of iPhoto lets you create new film rolls (select some photos and then choose File > Create Film Roll) and move photos from one roll to another (make sure you drag the photo(s) on top of the film roll's name—not just into the photo area). This is handy when you want to separate groups of non-related photos that were imported together or join two groups of related photos that were imported separately.

extra bits

- Click the triangle next to a film roll's name to hide its photos (or make them appear, if they were already hidden). Option-click any film roll's triangle to display or hide the contents of all the film rolls in your Library.

- Film rolls are only visible when you've selected the Library or a smart album (which we'll get to at the beginning of the next chapter) in the Source list.

- A film roll is dated on the day its photos are imported, not when they were taken, scanned, or emailed to you. The photos may thus have different dates than the film roll. You can change a film roll's date—to one that more closely reflects its photos' dates— by selecting the film roll, clicking the info button, and specifying a new date in the Information pane.

- When you sort by film rolls, the film rolls are first sorted according to their own dates, and then by the dates of the photos that they contain. The title of the film roll is not used in sorting. The order is not always instantly updated when you change the dates of a film roll's photos. In that case, sort the library by another criteria and then go back to sorting by film rolls to update the view.

- You may also sort your library according to keywords, titles, and the date, all of which we'll get to shortly. If you do so, the division into film rolls will not be visible.

increase viewing size p. 5

- Another way to see more photos at once is to turn off the automatic grid that requires that each photo occupy the same space as its neighbor, despite having a different orientation or size. Choose iPhoto > Preferences, click the Appearance tab at the top of the window, and then uncheck the Align photos to grid option.

- If you increase the viewing size too much, iPhoto can get downright sluggish. Press the number 2 on your keyboard to view your photos at what iPhoto considers the optimum size. (This is the size at which iPhoto has cached the thumbnails and so can display them more quickly.) Press the 1 to view them at maximum size.

rotate photos p. 6

- You can also rotate photos by choosing Photos > Rotate Clockwise (or Counter Clockwise), or by using the keyboard shortcuts Command-R and Command - Option-R.

- If you accidentally double-click a photo, you'll find yourself in Edit mode. Click the Done button to return to the main iPhoto window.

- Use standard Macintosh selection shortcuts to choose more than one photo. That is, click the first photo and then hold down the Shift key while you click a second photo to select the first, the second, and all the photos in between those two. Or, click the first photo and then hold down the Command key (with the Apple) while you select the second photo. This time, the ones in between stay unselected. Continue Command-clicking to add additional individual photos.

- If you find you often rotate your photos one way but not the other, you can change the default rotation direction in the Preferences dialog box. Choose iPhoto > Preferences, and then click the General tab at the top of the window. Choose the direction next to Rotate that you use most often. You can always Option-click the Rotate button when you need to rotate photos the other way.

- Rotate photos as you review them (as described on page 7) by using the same keyboard shortcuts described above or by clicking the controls on the screen.

review your photos p. 7

- Using the Play key in the lower-left corner of iPhoto's window runs a sort of simplified slideshow. We'll go into slideshows in more detail in Chapter 3.

- Click anywhere outside of the control area to stop reviewing the photos immediately. Otherwise, all of the selected photos will be shown before you return to the iPhoto window.

- Press the spacebar on your keyboard to pause the photo review. Press it again to resume.

- Press the right and left arrow keys on your keyboard to move through your photos, whether or not the controls are visible on screen. (If they weren't already visible, an abbreviated set of controls appears when you press either of the arrow keys.)

- You can press the up or down arrow to speed up or slow down the photo review, respectively.

- Keep the mouse still to make the controls disappear again.

- You can apply ratings while you're reviewing photos. Type a number from 1 to 5 to apply from one to five stars to the photo. Or type 0 to remove a rating. For more about rating photos, see page 11.

extra bits

get rid of the bad ones p. 8

- You can also delete unwanted photos by selecting them and pressing the Delete key. Or you can Control-click them and choose Move to Trash.

- Removed photos can be recovered by digging around in the Trash, as described in the following section.

empty the trash p. 9

- Once you empty the Trash, the photos are gone for good. There is no undo.

- You can empty the Trash by Control-clicking the Trash icon and choosing Empty Trash.

- Remove a photo from the Trash by Control-clicking it and choosing Restore to Photo Library.

- You can also drag a photo out of the Trash right back to the Library. It will automatically go back into the roll to which it belonged.

- You can't drag a photo from the Trash directly to an album. You must first return it to the Library.

label your photos p. 10

- Labeling your photos makes them easier to search for, as we'll see on page 21.

- The title of a photo comes originally from its file name. When you change the photo's title, its file name is not affected.

- You can jump from any info field in one photo to the same info field in the next photo by pressing Command-] (right bracket). Use Command-[(left bracket) to move to the previous photo's corresponding info field. This is a great way to edit the information for a bunch of photos all at once.

- You can also use the info window to see the size, format, and date of your photos or film rolls.

- iPhoto sometimes uses titles and comments in photo book designs as automatic captions for your photos. Consult Appendix A for more details.

- Otherwise, comments can also be used to simply record more detail about the photo that you don't want to forget.

rate your photos p. 11

- You can search for photos with a given rating by using a smart album (as described on pages 32–33.)

- You can also view a photo's rating by clicking the info button.

importing and organizing photos

- Rate photos as you review them (as described on page 7) by typing 1–5 (without the Command key) to apply that many stars to a photo or type 0 to remove a photo's rating.

- I almost never use anything except the 4 and 5-star ratings. It's not worth it to me to distinguish the mediocre photos from the below-average ones.

organize with albums p. 12

- Albums in iPhoto are strictly virtual. That is, they reference the photos in the Library but the photos themselves don't move—they stay in the Library. That means if you remove a photo from an album, it is not also removed from the Library (or any other album in which it appears). However, if you remove a photo from the Library (see page 8), it is removed from all the albums to which it belonged.

- You may add the same photo to as many different albums as you like.

- You can drag photos from one album into another. They will then belong to both albums.

- iPhoto can create an album for you, using your criteria to select the desired photos. This is called a smart album, and is discussed in more detail on pages 32–33.

- The Last Roll and Last x Months entries in the Source list are subsets of the Library itself, not true albums. That means if you delete a photo from one of these Library subsets, it's as if you deleted it from the Library itself—and it goes in the Trash. You can change how many rolls or how many months are shown through the Preferences box.

- You can display the number of photos in each album by choosing File > Preferences and checking Show photo count for albums in the General pane.

- Delete albums by selecting their name in the Source list and pressing the Delete key. The photos are not removed from the Library (or from any other albums to which they belong).

drag new albums p. 14

- On page 3, you imported photos into your Library by dragging them from your hard disk, CD, or DVD to the main viewing area. If you drag them all the way to the Source list, iPhoto will create a new album for the newly imported photos.

- Another way to create a new album from selected photos is by choosing File > New Album From Selection.

extra bits

organize with folders p. 15

- While you can drag the albums into different orders and in and out of folders, you can't drag them above the folders in the Source list.

- You can tell when something is going inside a folder because the folder gets framed in black. If there is just a horizontal line, you're only dragging the item to a new location.

- You can nest folders within other folders.

- Perhaps a folder's most useful contribution is letting you store a book and/or slideshow together with the album that you used to create it. We'll revisit this point in the next two chapters.

define keywords p. 16

- If you select a keyword before pressing the Add button, the newly created keyword will appear directly after the selected one. Otherwise, the newly created keyword appears at the end of the list.

- The keywords at the top of the list in the Preferences box will also appear at the top of the list in the iPhoto window, and will be the most accessible. You can reorder the list by dragging the keywords to the desired positions.

- If you remove a keyword from the list, it is automatically removed from any photo to which it was applied. For more on applying keywords, see page 18.)

- If you rename a keyword, the new keyword is applied to the same photos as the old one was.

apply keywords p. 18

- To remove one keyword from one or more photos, hold down the Option key while you drag the photo(s) over the keyword to be removed.

- To remove all of the keywords from one or more photos, drag the photos over the Reset keyword.

- The checkmark keyword is a generic keyword that's useful for marking a bunch of photos temporarily.

- I find dragging photos to be a remarkably awkward way of applying keywords, especially when you're applying multiple keywords to multiple photos. There is currently no keyboard shortcut (although there was in iPhoto 4). I heartily recommend using Keyword Assistant, an extremely useful piece of software written by Ken Ferry which allows you to apply one or more keywords via the keyboard. You can find it at: http://homepage.mac.com/kenferry/software.html

- Keywords are added to a photo in the order in which you apply them. So if you first apply Catalonia and then Object, that's how they will be listed for that photo. There is currently no way to reorder a particular photo's keywords (short of removing them and applying them anew in the desired order).

search by keywords p. 19

- In version 5.0.2 and later, click more than one keyword to see only the photos that have both keywords. Regularly clicked keywords are blue. Hold down the Shift key to select more than one keyword to see the photos that have one keyword OR the other applied (or both). Shift-clicked keywords are displayed in purple.

- Option-click one or more keywords to find all the photos that do not have those keywords assigned. Option-clicked keywords are red.

- You can combine Option-clicked keywords with regular or Shift-clicked keywords. For example, click Catalonia and then Option-click Objects to find all the objects that do have Catalonia AND don't have Objects.

- Click the keyword again to remove the search request. Click the circled x next to Reset to remove all the keyword search requests.

- Searching by keyword automatically cancels a search by date or by text. To use more criteria, try a smart album (see pages 32–33).

search by date p. 20

- Command-click a previously chosen time period to deselect it (without deselecting any other chosen time periods).

- Double-click a day or click the blue dot at the beginning of the week to select an entire week.

- Option-click a month, week, or day to choose that month or day regardless of year. For example, if you want to see all the pictures from New Year's Day, you could Option-click January 1. Such year-independent time periods are displayed in purple.

- Hold down Shift along with the Option key to add contiguous days or months to your year-independent time period. Hold down Command along with the Option key to add non-contiguous days or months to your year-independent time period.

extra bits

- You can Command-click a year-independent time period to convert it to the time period for the given year.
- When you're viewing the individual days of a month, the forward arrow changes to a backward arrow. Click the backward arrow to return to the month view.
- Click the word Calendar itself at the top of the calendar to jump to the current year.
- Searching by date automatically cancels a search by text (page 21) or by keyword (page 19). To use more criteria, try a smart album (see pages 32–33).

search by text p. 21

- Notice in the example, that iPhoto starts searching from the very first letter and may find what you're looking for before you finish typing the first word.
- Searching by text automatically cancels a search by date (page 20) or by keyword (page 19). To use more criteria, try a smart album (see pages 32–33).

- If you type more than one word, iPhoto 5.0.2 (and presumably later versions) finds all the photos with both the first word AND the second. Versions 5 and 5.01 found photos with either the first OR the second. I think it's worth it to upgrade just for that.

sort your photos p. 22

- You can also sort your photos by film roll (if you're viewing the Library), by Title, by Date, or by Rating. And you can sort albums manually, as described on pages 34–35 and page 63.
- If you rate your photos as you review them, you can then put them in order of rating to quickly gather the best ones and make them into an album.
- Why, you might ask, are the keywords in different orders in the illustration on page 22? The answer is that keywords are added to a photo in the order that you apply them, and as of this writing, cannot be reordered. For more on applying keywords, see page 18.

importing and organizing photos

2. creating a photo book

The project that we'll create in this chapter is a professionally printed and bound photo book. (Of course, you don't have to actually send it to get printed—but you'll know how.)

Since the project shows pictures from a trip abroad, you'll use iPhoto's striking Travel book theme which features cream and orange backgrounds and passport-like stamps, right on the pages. You'll learn how to select photos from your iPhoto Library, organize them on pages, change page types and designs to suit your photos, rearrange photos and pages, and fix minor problems in your photos along the way. Finally, you'll learn how to send the files to Apple and order your printed book.

choose photos for book

Once your photos are imported and adequately labeled, use a smart album to help filter in the photos you want. To start, choose File > New Smart Album.

File	Edit	Photos	Share	View	Wi
New Album...					⌘N
New Book					
New Slideshow					
New Album From Selection...					⇧⌘N
New Smart Album...					⌥⌘N
New Folder					
Create Film Roll					
Add to Library...					⌘O
Close Window					⌘W
Edit Smart Album					
Page Setup...					⇧⌘P
Print...					⌘P

First give your smart album a name. Then, choose any to throw a wider net for photos that might fulfill one condition but not necessarily the others. Choose all to require that each photo fulfills each and every one of the specified conditions.

Click the plus sign (+) to add additional conditions to your smart album. The minus sign (-) removes conditions.

Smart Album name: Catalonia Book

Match [any] of the following conditions:

Roll	contains	boquería	⊖ ⊕
Roll	contains	guell	⊖ ⊕
Roll	contains	tower	⊖ ⊕
Roll	contains	pedrera	⊖ ⊕
Roll	contains	sagrada	⊖ ⊕

(Cancel) (OK)

Set up the conditions by choosing the criteria in the various pop-up menus.

Click OK when you're ready to have iPhoto perform the search and place the photos that pass your conditions in your new album.

creating a photo book

The smart album will contain only those photos that satisfy the conditions you specified on the previous page.

creating a photo book

put photos in order

While you can sort the photos in a smart album by date, keyword, title, or rating, you cannot organize them your own way—which is pretty key when creating a photo book. To take advantage of the smart album's filtering without losing the ability to sort your own way, you'll transfer the photos from the smart album into a new regular album. Start by clicking the smart album and choosing Edit > Select All.

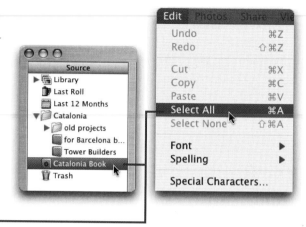

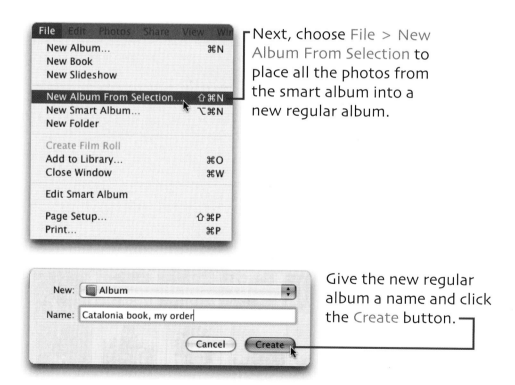

Next, choose File > New Album From Selection to place all the photos from the smart album into a new regular album.

Give the new regular album a name and click the Create button.

Click on the photo that you want to have appear at the beginning of your book and drag it to the top of the album. The vertical black bar indicates where the photo will go.

Continue dragging until all the similar photos are grouped together (or in the way that you'd like them to appear in the book). I've provided the exact order I use for this project on the web site, if you'd like to follow along (see page xiii).

choose a book theme

With your desired album selected, click the Book button at the bottom of the iPhoto window.

The default option for Book Type is Large - 11" x 8 ½" (in hardcover, though that's not immediately obvious). Other possible types are softcover in large, medium, and small.

Each book theme contains different page designs. Picture Book, for example, has page designs that accommodate up to 16 pictures on a page but little text; Travel offers combinations of text and smaller quantities of photos with stamps, postcards, and other travel motifs. For a complete description of each book theme, see Appendix A. For this example, click the Travel theme.

The Options + Prices button takes you to Apple's web site where they explain how much each book costs. Our large hardcover book will cost $29.99 with 20 double-sided pages, not counting shipping and handling.

We'll leave the Double-sided pages option as is. You can, however, uncheck it to lay out large, hardcover books on single-sided, higher quality pages.

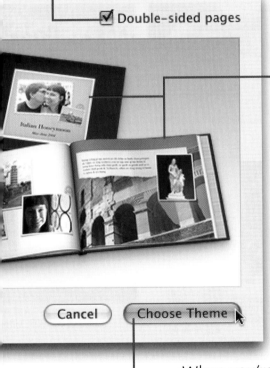

☑ Double–sided pages

When you choose a theme, you'll see a sample of a few pages, along with the cover. I don't think there's enough information to make an informed choice. That's why I provide more details about each theme in Appendix A.

Cancel Choose Theme

When you're satisfied with your choices, click Choose Theme to begin your photo book.

creating a photo book

use the book mode

After you click the Choose Theme button on the previous page, iPhoto gives you information about automatically placing your photos. Click OK.

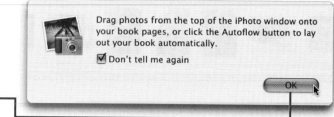

Drag photos from the top of the iPhoto window onto your book pages, or click the Autoflow button to lay out your book automatically.

☑ Don't tell me again

OK

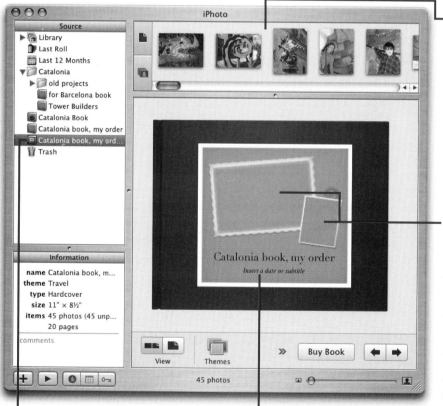

In Book mode, iPhoto places the photos from the selected album, in order, across the top of the window in an area known as the photo browser.

The first layout you'll see is the cover, which in the Travel theme has frames for two photos. Frames yet to be filled in iPhoto are shown with a gray background.

A new book appears in your Source list, with the same name as the album from which it was generated. Notice the book icon to the left of its name.

The default name for your book comes from the name of the album you selected. We'll change it shortly.

organize the book files

To better keep track of the book and the albums we used to create it, we'll create a new folder and store all three items inside. Start by choosing File > New Folder.

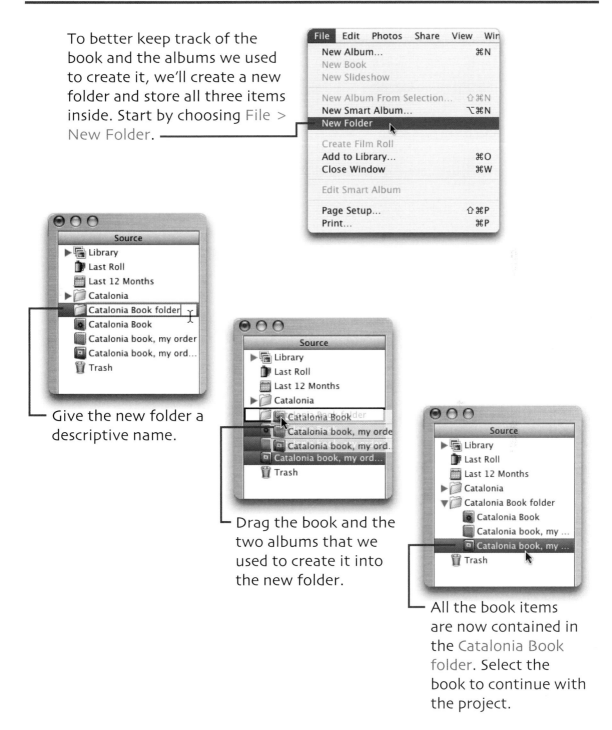

Give the new folder a descriptive name.

Drag the book and the two albums that we used to create it into the new folder.

All the book items are now contained in the Catalonia Book folder. Select the book to continue with the project.

place photos on cover

Drag the desired photo from the photo browser to the frame where it should go on the page.

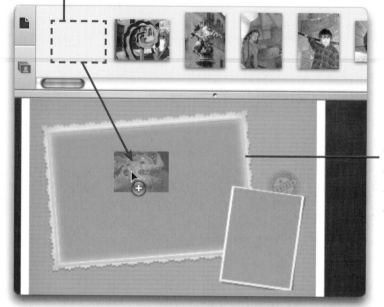

You can tell which frame the photo will go into by the yellow outline.

The chosen photo disappears from the photo browser and fills the selected frame.

creating a photo book

For the second photo on the cover, we'll drag a horizontal photo to a vertical frame.

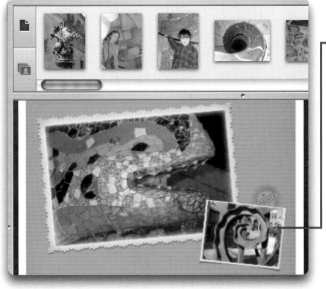

In this example, iPhoto changes the frame to suit the photograph. In some other page designs, however, iPhoto crops the photo to suit the frame.

magnify the view

It'll be easier to edit the cover title if we zoom in to get a better look. The zoom controls are at the bottom right of the window.

Drag the blue ball in the zoom control toward the right to magnify the view.

You may need to drag the blue scroll bars to center the area of interest on the page, depending on how large your window is.

The text is now big and clear and easy to edit.

edit text

Select or click in the text on the cover that you wish to change.

The text block that will be affected is outlined in blue.

Choose Edit > Font > Show Fonts to open the Macintosh OS X standard Font dialog box. Select the desired font, typeface, and size from the lists. You can also choose a color, underscore, and shadow style. Changes are applied immediately.

Font

Collections	Family	Typeface	Size
All Fonts	Baskerville	Regular	40
Favorites	Big Caslon	Italic	9
Recently Used	Cochin	Bold	10
Chinese	Copperplate	Bold Italic	11
Classic	Didot		12
Fixed Width			13
Fun			14
Japanese			18
Korean			24
Modern			36
New-0			48
PDF			64
Web			72
			96
			144
			288

315°

Search

I chose 40-point Cochin Regular in Cayenne Red for the main title, and 24-point Cochin Italic in black for the subhead.

navigate to next page

When you start a new book, the photo browser at the top of the Book view shows the available photos for the book. ⌐

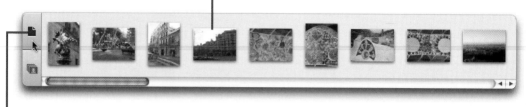

Click the page view icon to have the photo browser show the proposed layout for this book.

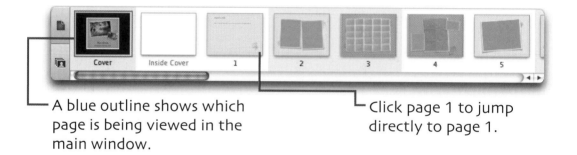

A blue outline shows which page is being viewed in the main window.

Click page 1 to jump directly to page 1.

You can also click the arrows at the bottom of the Book view to navigate through the book, page by page.

change the page type

All iPhoto books start with an
introduction page on page 1.

I don't want a text introduction in
this book, so we'll change it to a one-
photo page. The Page Type menu,
which varies depending on the book
theme you've chosen, lets you specify
how many photos should appear on
the page. Choose One to apply a one-
photo page to page 1 of this book.

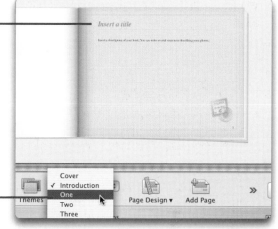

The big gray frame indicates how the
photo will be laid out, once you drag
it in. In this case, the photo will fill
the page.

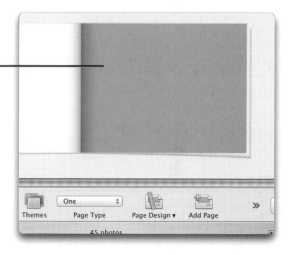

Drag the next photo (of Saint
George), into the gray frame on
page 1. iPhoto crops the vertically
oriented photo automatically to fill
the frame. (Compare this behavior
with how iPhoto changed the frame
to fit the orientation on the cover.)

creating a photo book

fix red eye

Navigate to page 2 and drag the next two pictures (of the girl and boy) to the gray frames. —

Drag the zoom controls to magnify the view. —

Because the pictures were taken with flash in a dark place (the stairwell of the Sagrada Família church in Barcelona), they suffer from red eye, where the light reflects from the back of the eye, which is covered with blood vessels.

Control-click the left photo and choose Edit Photo from the pop-up menu. —

iPhoto displays the photo in Edit mode.

Magnify the area around the eyes by dragging the zoom control toward the right.

Click the Red-Eye tool at the bottom of the Edit mode window.

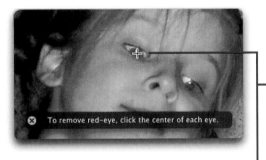

With the Red-Eye tool active, click the center of each red eye.

When you've finished fixing the red eyes, click the Red-Eye tool again. Click Done to return to Book mode.

On your own: Fix the boy's eyes.

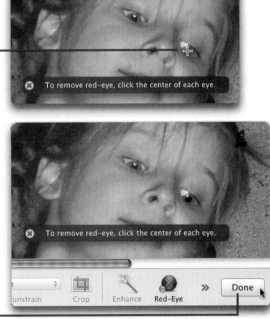

creating a photo book

enlarge and center

The photo on the left was taken from just a bit farther away so the girl appears a little smaller than the boy on the right.

Double-click the photo to reveal the zoom bar. Drag the slider to the right to blow up the picture.

While the zoom bar is still showing, drag the mouse in the picture to recenter it. (The pointer turns into a hand.)

creating a photo book

view a two-page spread

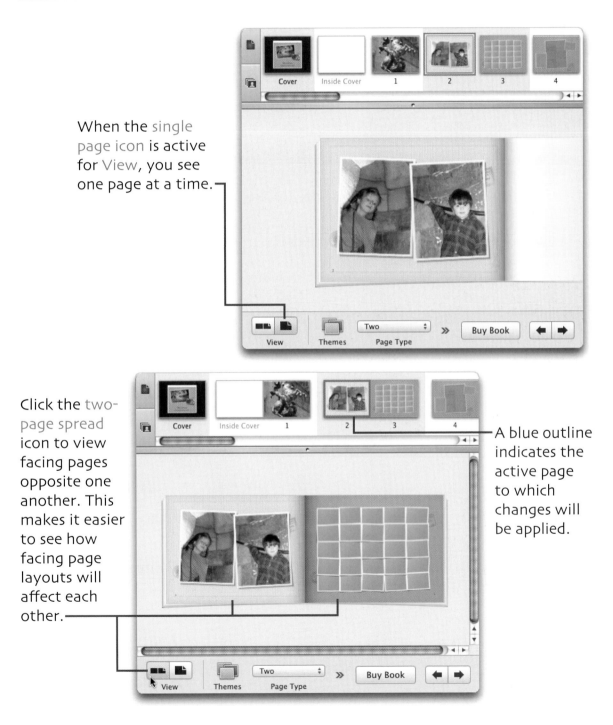

When the single page icon is active for View, you see one page at a time.

Click the two-page spread icon to view facing pages opposite one another. This makes it easier to see how facing page layouts will affect each other.

A blue outline indicates the active page to which changes will be applied.

change page design

I've dragged the next photo to the right-hand page, but I don't like the mosaic effect. ─────

The Page Design pop-up menu (the title is unfortunately hidden in this illustration) changes depending on what you've selected for Themes and Page Type. Here, we see there are five different page designs for the Travel theme's one-photo page. ─────

The placement of the gray frame on the page shows how the photo will be laid out on the page. Choose option 2 to display the photo, slightly rotated, in the middle of the page. ─┐

The currently selected page design is indicated with a checkmark. ─┐

creating a photo book

I think this page design works much better
with this layout. ———————————

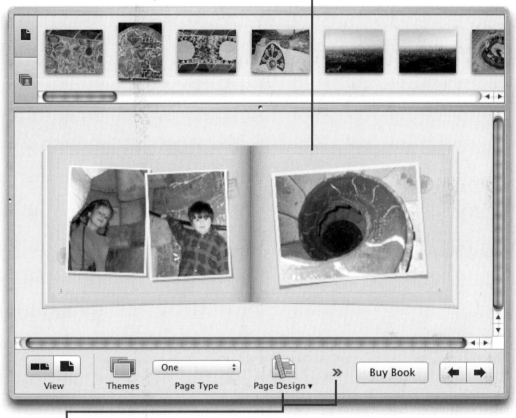

The Page Design icon lives at the bottom of the Book mode
window to the right of the Page Type menu. However, if you
make the window too narrow, it can disappear from view (as
will other tools). In that case, click the double-right arrow (»)
and choose Page Design (or the tool that you need) from the
pop-up menu that appears.

rearrange photos

On page 4, you'll find one of iPhoto's special page designs. It appears by default, cannot be chosen in the Page Design menu, and requires particular care: You must drag the vertically oriented photo to the middle frame first, and then fill the other frames. Otherwise, the design automatically switches to the regular layout.

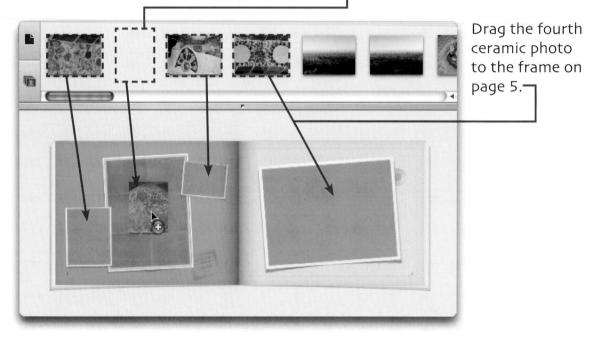

Drag the fourth ceramic photo to the frame on page 5.

It seems like the detailed photo on the right would work better on the left-hand page, instead of the wider view of the bench that is there currently.

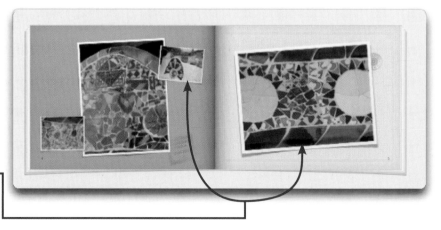

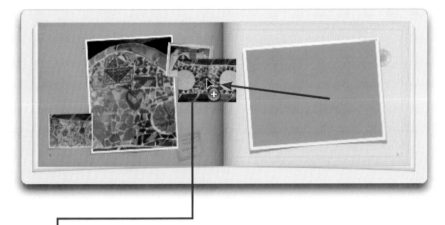

Drag the photo from page 5 over to the top-right frame on page 4 to switch the two photos. You'll know you're close enough when the target frame is outlined in yellow.

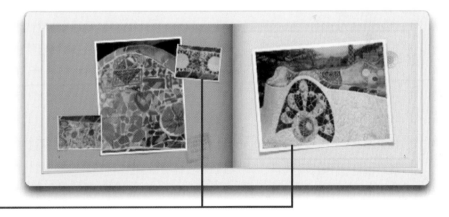

This layout makes more sense. The three detailed photos are together on the left page while the larger overview photo gets better treatment on the right.

create a panorama

Place the next two photos (two halves of a panoramic view of Barcelona) and choose the full page design for both pages.

The new Water Company tower in Barcelona (among other things) is repeated in both photographs.

Double-click the left photo to make the zoom control appear. Then drag the slider slightly more than half way across to blow up the image.

Enlarge the right photo the same way. You can see that the middle area still repeats.

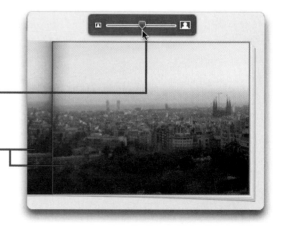

creating a photo book

Return to the left photo and double-click it again. Ignore the zoom control. Instead, place the pointer within the photo, click, and drag. The pointer turns into a hand. Drag (pan) the photo to the right and down.

The tower is now almost in the center of the book.

Finally, double-click the right photo and drag it to the left until it lines up with the left photo. You may need to adjust the zoom slightly until they match.

Because the center portion will be somewhat hidden in the spine of the book, you don't have to be pixel-precise when lining up the photos.

creating a photo book

drag to change design

Here I've already dragged two photos to page 8 and one to the frame in page 9.

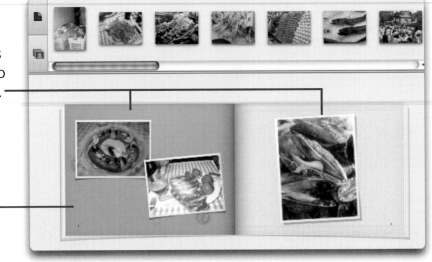

For each book theme, iPhoto offers a single default layout, which relies heavily on one- and two-photo designs. (You can view each book theme's default layout in Appendix A.)

When you drag a new photo to an empty part of a page...

...iPhoto automatically changes the page design to accommodate the new photo.

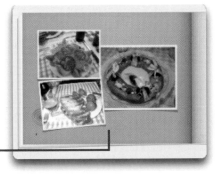

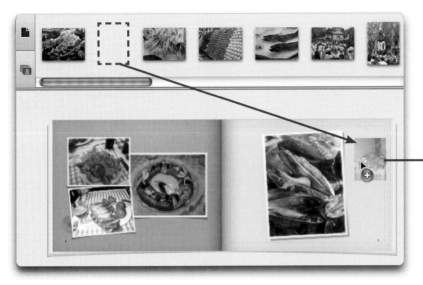

It doesn't matter which bit of empty space on the page you drag the new photo to...

...iPhoto always puts the new photo in what it considers the next available space.

Of course, you can drag the left one over the right (until its frame is outlined in yellow) to rearrange them.

control overlapping

Start by dragging the next three photos into the layout on page 10.

iPhoto tucks the top one behind the right one but in front of the left one.

Control-click the top photo (note the blue outline when it is selected) and choose Move to Front from the pop-up menu that appears.

The top photo is now on top of both of the other photos.

creating a photo book

remove photos

Control-click a photo and choose Remove Photo in the pop-up menu...

Or, select a photo and press the Delete key on your keyboard...

...to remove a photo—but not its frame—from a page.

In both cases, the photo is returned to the book's photo browser.

On your own: Place the last two food photos on page 11.

autoflow the photos

When there are photos in the photo browser, the Autoflow button tells iPhoto to place the photos into the pages that have not yet been laid out.

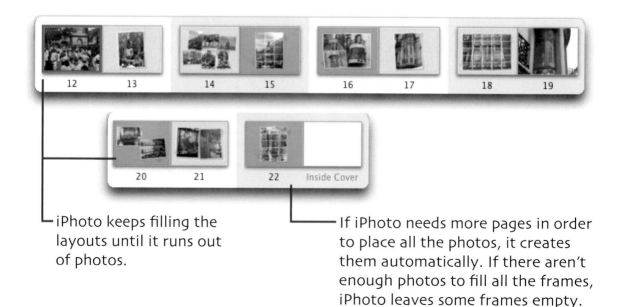

iPhoto keeps filling the layouts until it runs out of photos.

If iPhoto needs more pages in order to place all the photos, it creates them automatically. If there aren't enough photos to fill all the frames, iPhoto leaves some frames empty.

creating a photo book

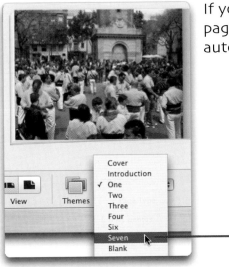

If you change the
page design after you
autoflow the photos...

...iPhoto does not
automatically reflow them
for you.

But when you choose
Autoflow a second time
(as long as there are no
more photos in the photo
browser)...

...iPhoto reflows the photos into
the layouts throughout your
book—without reordering the
pictures—so that there are no
blank frames on any page.

On your own: Change the Page Type on page 13 of the photo book to a
two-photo page and then click Autoflow to reflow the book. Then look over
iPhoto's autoflowing handiwork on pages 14–17.

creating a photo book

add photos to book

To add more photos to your book from another album or film roll, first, select that album or film roll.

Select the photos you want to add and drag them to the book you're working on (not the album that you made the book from).

The added photos appear at the beginning of the photo browser and are ready to be placed.

creating a photo book

finish placing photos

Drag the photo of the magical rooftop of Antoni Gaudí's Pedrera to page 18 and change the page design so that it fills the page.

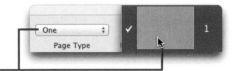

Change the page type on page 19 to a three-photo page and then place the three modernist chimneys in it.

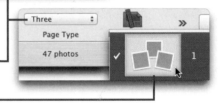

Finally, change the page type for page 20 to a two-photo page, and then choose this wonderful page design that makes it look as if there is a photograph lying on the sidewalk tile.

We'll remove this extra page shortly.

reorder pages

The spread on pages 18–19 is so nice, it should go at the front of the book. To move it there, first make sure the photo browser is on page view (by clicking the page view icon).

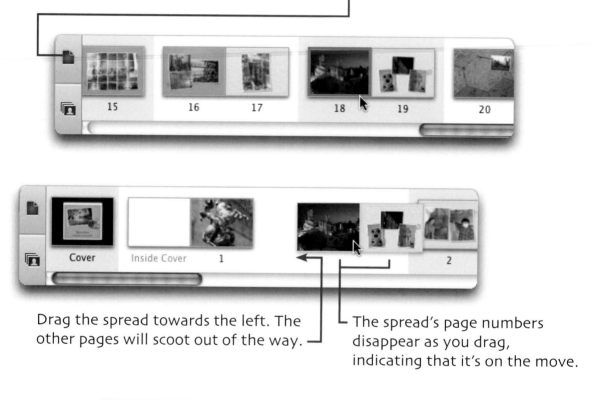

Drag the spread towards the left. The other pages will scoot out of the way.

The spread's page numbers disappear as you drag, indicating that it's on the move.

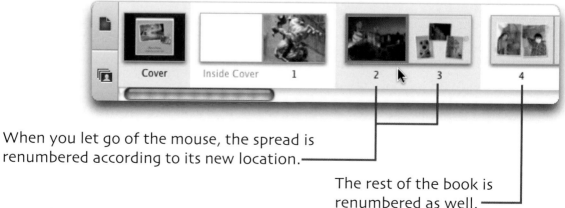

When you let go of the mouse, the spread is renumbered according to its new location.

The rest of the book is renumbered as well.

remove pages

To remove the extra pages that iPhoto added when we did the autoflow (see pages 60–61), we'll start by selecting the first such page in the photo browser.

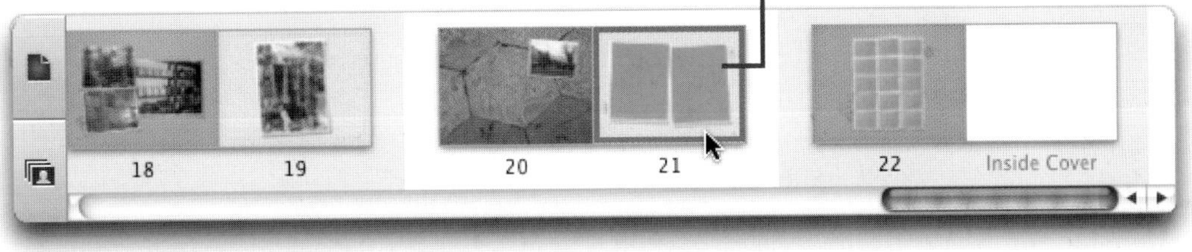

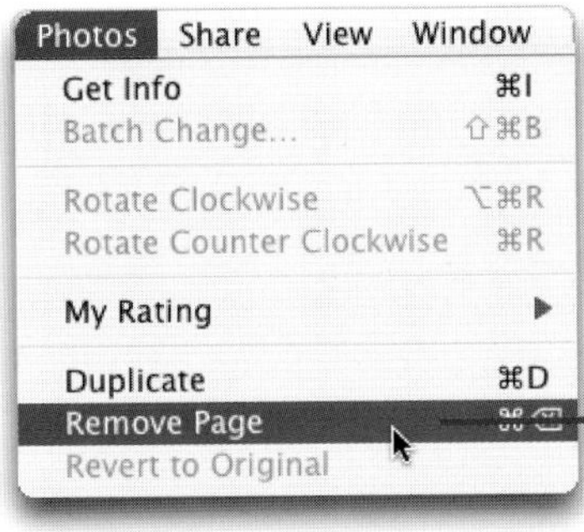

Then, choose Remove Page from the Photos menu.

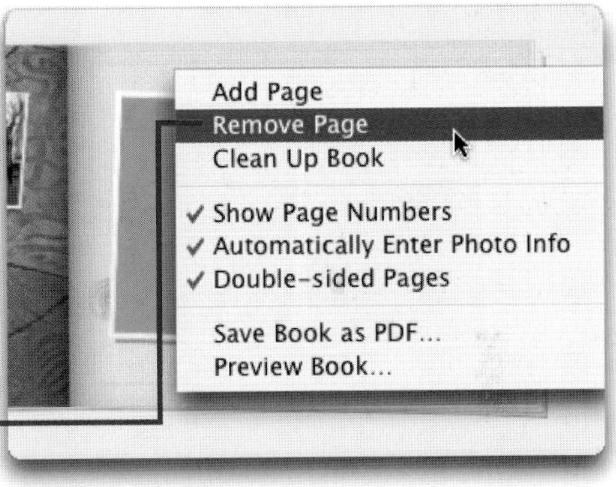

Or Control-click the page and choose Remove Page from the the pop-up menu that appears.

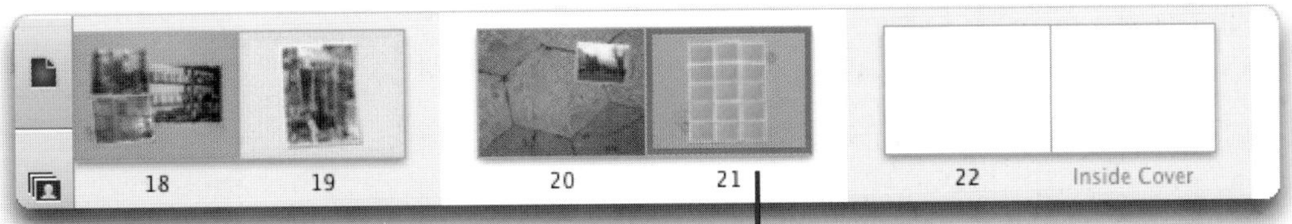

The page is removed from the layout and the pages that followed it move up to fill its place.

On your own: Remove the remaining extra empty pages.

order book

1 When you're finished laying out the book and ready to get it printed and bound, click the Buy Book button at the bottom of the Book view.

2 iPhoto creates a PDF file of your book.

3 iPhoto then connects to Apple via the Internet to process the book order.

4 The Book Type that you chose back on page 36 is shown here. Make sure this is what you want.

5 You'll see the preliminary cost of the book, based on the number of pages.

6 Before going further, you have to sign in to your Apple account or create a new one if you don't have one. Click the Set Up Account button either way.

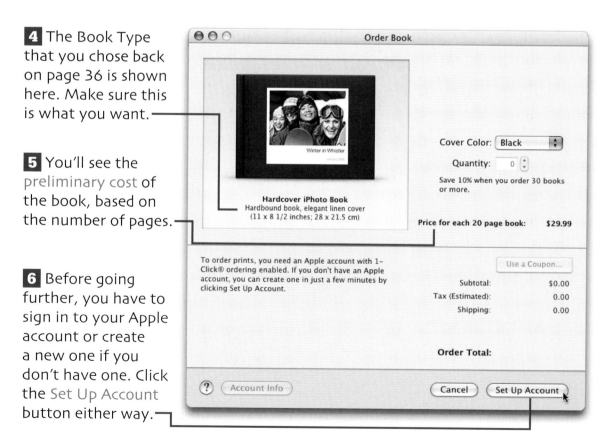

creating a photo book

Set Up Account

Apple Account Sign-in

To continue with your order, enter an Apple ID and Password. If you don't have an Apple account, create one.

Create Account   Learn More

Apple ID: barcelona@visca.com   Example: steve@mac.com

Password: •••••••••••   Forgot Password?

Cancel   Sign In

7 Enter your Apple ID and Password and click Sign In. (Or click Create Account if you don't have an Apple account yet.)

Order Book

Winter in Whistler

Cover Color: Black

Quantity: 1

Save 10% when you order 30 books or more.

Hardcover iPhoto Book
Hardbound book, elegant linen cover
(11 x 8 1/2 inches; 28 x 21.5 cm)

Price for each 20 page book: $29.99

Account: barcelona@visca.com (1-Click® enabled)   Use a Coupon...

Ship To: Myself   Subtotal: $29.99

Tax (Estimated):   1.50

Ship Via: Standard   Shipping: 7.99

Usually ships in 3–4 days.

Book availability is based on your United States billing address. Pricing is in US Dollars.   Order Total: $39.48

? Account Info   Cancel   Buy Now

8 You can now review the shipping costs and full price for your order.

9 The Buy Now button becomes active. Click it to finalize your order. The PDF file of your book is sent to Apple. You'll receive a confirmation of your order via email and the actual, printed book will arrive in a week or so, depending on where you are.

creating a photo book

extra bits

choose a book theme p. 36

- The themes are very similar for large and medium books. They are simply reduced in size in the medium book. All themes are available both in large (hardcover or softcover) and medium sizes. The only theme for small books is Picture Book with just one photo per page. For more details, see Appendix A.

organize the book files p. 39

- You can't create a folder with the same name as any other item, even if it's enclosed within another folder.
- You can hide the contents of a folder by clicking the triangle to its left. Reveal a folder's contents by clicking the triangle again.

edit text p. 43

- There is a Settings button to the far right of the toolbar at the bottom of the window which gives you access to the default fonts that iPhoto uses for each book theme. I (and others) have found it to be extremely buggy as of version 5.0.2, routinely applying a different font than the one chosen. I recommend avoiding the Settings box altogether.

- If you type too much text and/or make it too big for its box, iPhoto will display a yellow warning triangle near the text. Either reduce the size or the quantity of text until the triangle disappears.

navigate to next page p. 44

- You can also use the arrow keys on your keyboard to move from one page to another.

change the page type p. 45

- If you don't want iPhoto to automatically crop your photo, you can Control-click the photo and choose Fit Photo to Frame Size. For more details, see page 139.
- If you choose a page type with fewer photos than the current one, any extra photos will be returned to the photo browser.

fix red eye p. 46

- If you don't like the results, choose Edit > Undo before you click the Done button, or Control-click the photo in Edit mode at any time and choose Revert to Original to remove all edits.

enlarge and center p. 48

- Once you can see the zoom slider, you can then double-click the photo again to get into Edit mode.

- You can't move a picture around in its box unless it is bigger than the box, either because iPhoto fit it into a box of a different orientation (as on page 45), or because you've just enlarged it.

- Enlarging a picture this way, in contrast with cropping a photo as described on pages 80–81, does not affect the way the photo appears in any other book or slideshow.

change page design p. 50

- Not all page types have distinct page designs from which to choose. In Appendix A, you'll find each book theme's page types along with the page designs that correspond to each one.

rearrange photos p. 52

- The three-photo design that iPhoto offers by default on page 4 of the Travel theme is tricky. If you drag a photo to one of the lateral frames first, the layout will change to the regular three-photo page design (without the large creased central photo). If that happens, the only way to get back to the special page design is to choose Edit > Undo.

- Of course, you may not like that creased effect, in which case you can drag the photos any way you like and smile when it disappears.

- Sometimes iPhoto changes the design when you rearrange photos, especially when you are mixing horizontal and vertical photos. See Appendix A for examples.

- In this example, the result would be the same if you dragged the photo on page 4 on top of the photo in page 5.

create a panorama p. 54

- If you zoom in too far, you'll see a small yellow warning triangle in the upper-right corner. This means that the photo may appear pixelated when you print it, or in layman's terms, that you've blown it up too big. Drag back to the left a little until the yellow triangle disappears.

- The zoom control appears when you double-click the photo. If you double-click again, you'll jump to Edit mode (where you can click Done to return to Book view). The pan hand does not appear until you drag (after double-clicking).

control overlapping p. 58

- If the Move to Front command does not appear when you Control-click, it may be that you're Control-clicking the page and not the photo.

extra bits

- In the Travel theme you can use Send to Back to make the photos go behind the little passport stamps that are part of the design of the book.

remove photos p. 59

- You can remove a photo from a book entirely by selecting it in the photo browser (not on a layout) and pressing the Delete key.

autoflow the photos p. 60

- If there are photos in the photo browser when you use Autoflow, these photos are placed on new pages and do not fill empty frames on earlier pages.

- If there are no photos in the photo browser when you use Autoflow, iPhoto reflows the entire book in order to fill every frame on every page while maintaining the current order of the photos. If you don't like the results, you can always choose Edit > Undo.

- The Autoflow command often places photos in a different order than you'd expect. For example, in the Travel theme two-photo page, it puts the first photo on the right and the second on the left. But in the three-photo page, it places the photos from left to right. On the seven-photo page, as you can see

in the example, it places the first photo in the lower-right corner, the second in the upper-left corner, the third in the upper-right corner, the fourth in the lower-left corner, the fifth in the center, the sixth in the upper-center and the seventh in the lower-center!

- If you don't see the Autoflow button, it may be hidden because your window is too narrow. In such a case, you can choose Autoflow from the >> menu that replaced it. Also see page 51 for more details.

- The Clean Up Book command, which appears when you Control-click an iPhoto book page, was almost identical to the Autoflow button in version 5.0.1. However, instead of leaving empty frames on earlier pages empty, it removed them entirely, changing page designs as necessary. In version 5.0.2 (and presumably later versions), the Clean Up Book command only removes empty frames from half-filled pages, but does not fill or otherwise affect any empty pages.

- I should note that I counted and ordered the photos that would be flowed onto pages 14–17 ahead of time so that they would look nice when they were autoflowed. Indeed, that's a good way to use the Autoflow button: study the

creating a photo book

default layout that iPhoto creates (detailed in Appendix A), choose the right number of photos for each page and then let iPhoto place them all.

finish placing photos p. 63

- iPhoto does not choose a selection of page types and designs to suit your photographs. Instead, it has a default layout pattern for each book theme which it always applies. (You can find all of the book theme's default layouts illustrated in Appendix A.) For some curious reason, iPhoto doesn't use some of its nicest page designs in these layouts. For example, the two-photo design used on page 20 of the project in this book and a four-photo postcard page, among others, are not part of the default layout for the Travel theme. Be sure to look through Appendix A and explore all the page types and designs.

reorder pages p. 64

- If you're not viewing the pages of the book as facing pages (see page 49), you can reorder individual pages. For example, if you want to switch the order of two pages in a spread, you'd have to first click the single page view, and then drag the right page towards the left in the photo browser.

remove pages p. 65

- If the page that you remove contained photos, these are returned unharmed to the photo browser.

- You can also add pages. Either click the Add Page button at the bottom of the Book window or Control-click a page and choose Add Page from the pop-up menu that appears. If you're viewing two-page spreads (see page 49), you'll get two new pages. If you're viewing individual pages, you'll just get one new page.

- It would be nice if the Clean Up Book command that appears when you Control-click a page actually got rid of your empty pages, but alas, it does not. Instead it only removes the empty photo frames from half-filled pages. It does not affect completely empty pages in the slightest.

- If you like, you can add photos to the empty pages instead of removing them. While iPhoto books must have at least 20 pages, they can have up to one hundred.

extra bits

order book p. 66

- You must have an Apple account in order to buy a book.

- iPhoto indicates problems on your pages with yellow warning triangles and won't let you order a book until you resolve the associated problems. If you find a yellow triangle near a photo, it means the photo has either been blown up too much (see page 48) or simply had too low of a resolution to start with to print well at the size you've set it. You can reduce the size or choose another shot. If you find a yellow triangle near text, it means that the text is either too big for the box it's in or there's a problem with the font. Edit the text as necessary (see page 43) until the triangle disappears.

- You can print out the pages on your own printer, but it's hard to match the quality of a bound book with photos that bleed all the way to the edge.

- iPhoto will not let you print a book that has empty frames. You'll either have to fill them manually, use Autoflow, or change the Page Type for those pages.

- If you don't change the default text in a layout, iPhoto will warn you that default text will not be printed.

- You can find and view the PDF file that Apple creates of your book. From the Finder, choose Find. Then set the criteria as Name is iPhoto and Visibility is invisible items. You'll find a PDF of your book inside an invisible folder called iPhoto.

- Currently, iPhoto creates your PDF files at 150 dpi. Some clever folks on the iPhoto discussion board at Apple (http://discussions. info.apple.com) found out how to improve the quality of the printed book by changing the output dpi to 300 dpi. First quit iPhoto. Then, find the com.apple.iPhoto.plist file inside your Preferences folder. Make a copy of it and store it somewhere safe in case you need to restore the original. Then open the plist file with a text editor. Search for BookTargetImageDPI, and change the setting from 150 to 300. Save changes and return to iPhoto. Any book that you create from now on will have an output resolution of 300 dpi. This file will be larger and take longer to upload to Apple than the 150 dpi version, but it will also print better.

creating a photo book

3. making a slideshow

One of the great promises of digital photography is that you can save a fortune by only printing the good ones. iPhoto makes it so that you don't even have to print those: you can make spectacular slideshows out of your digital still shots.

In this chapter, you'll learn how to select a group of photos for a slideshow, crop them to fit the screen on which you'll show them, zoom in and pan from one point to another à la Ken Burns, link them together with stunning transitions, and lastly, add music as a final touch. You can then view your slideshow right on your Mac's screen, watch them on television, or export them to a DVD.

import photos

Download the photos for this chapter from the web site (xiii) and then drag the folder of photos to the Source list in iPhoto to import them into your iPhoto Library.

A new album is automatically created in the Source list with the same name as the folder in the Finder and with all the photos that the folder contained.

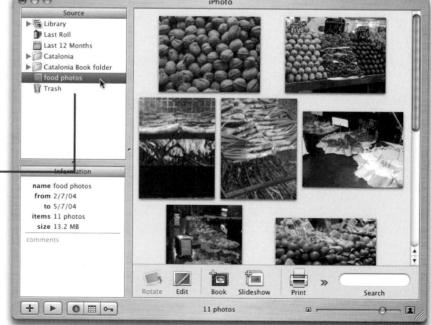

put photos in order

Start by dragging the blue size control to the left so that you can see more photos at once.

We want to put similarly themed photos together. First, select the third and fourth photos and drag them to the front of the list.

The black vertical bar indicates where the photos will be moved.

The red outlined number indicates how many photos you're dragging.

The moved photos now appear at the beginning of the list.

On your own: Finish sorting the photos into groups: after the onions come tapas, then fruit and vegetables. You can find the exact sorting order used for the project in this chapter on the web site (see page xiii).

making a slideshow

create a slideshow

Creating a slideshow couldn't be much simpler. Select the food photos album that contains the pictures that should be in the slideshow and then click the Slideshow button at the bottom of the iPhoto window.

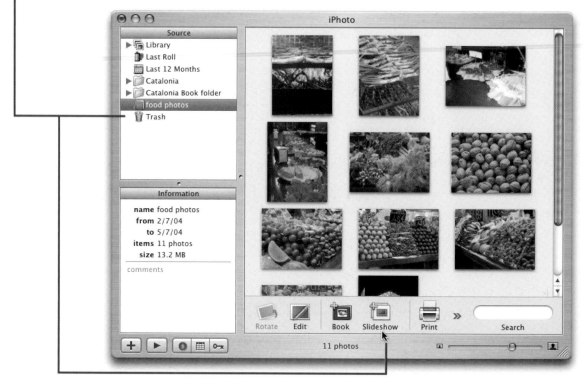

The new slideshow is created in the Source list. Its name comes from the album from which it was generated.

Select the slideshow in the Source list to enter Slideshow mode (shown opposite), where you can customize your slideshow.

The slideshow's contents are displayed across the top of the slideshow window, in the photo browser.

Drag the separator bar to make the photo browser (and its contents) bigger or smaller.

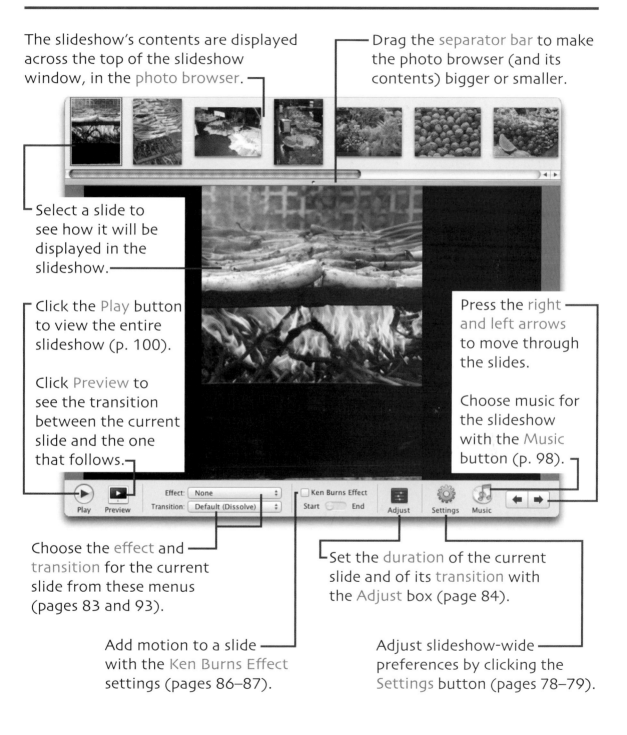

Select a slide to see how it will be displayed in the slideshow.

Press the right and left arrows to move through the slides.

Click the Play button to view the entire slideshow (p. 100).

Click Preview to see the transition between the current slide and the one that follows.

Choose music for the slideshow with the Music button (p. 98).

Choose the effect and transition for the current slide from these menus (pages 83 and 93).

Set the duration of the current slide and of its transition with the Adjust box (page 84).

Add motion to a slide with the Ken Burns Effect settings (pages 86–87).

Adjust slideshow-wide preferences by clicking the Settings button (pages 78–79).

making a slideshow

adjust default settings

To change default settings for the entire slideshow, click the Settings button at the bottom of the Slideshow window.

Enter the number 3 to play each slide for 3 seconds.

Change the default Transition to Wipe to have each slide gradually cover over the previous one. Choose the upper arrow to have the wipe effect move from bottom to top.

Leave the default Speed of the transition in the middle position.

You'll see a preview of the effect in the box. Here you can see the second photo in the slideshow gradually wiping out the first, from bottom to top.

Default Settings for the entire slideshow

Play each slide for [3] seconds

Transition: [Wipe]
Speed: ———

☑ Repeat slideshow
☐ Scale photos to fill screen
☑ Automatic Ken Burns Effect
☐ Show titles
☐ Show my ratings
☐ Show slideshow controls

◉ Repeat music during slideshow
The music will repeat for as long as the slides play.

◯ Fit slideshow to music
Slide durations will be adjusted to make the slides play for as long as the music plays.

Slideshow Format: [Current Display]

[Cancel]   [OK]

Don't click the OK button until you make the changes on the following page.

making a slideshow

iPhoto automatically applies the Ken Burns Effect (named after the documentary director who popularized the technique of panning and zooming in on still shots) to all the photos in your slideshow. For this project, you'll apply the effect more selectively, so you'll need to deselect this box.

You need to tell iPhoto where you'll ultimately display your slideshow so that your slides will fill the chosen screen, without leaving any unsightly black bars on the edges. This project is designed to be displayed on a TV screen, so choose 4:3 iDVD, TV in the Slideshow Format menu.

Default Settings for the entire slideshow

Play each slide for [3] ⬍ seconds

Transition: [Wipe ▼]
Speed: ───────○────

☑ Repeat slideshow
☐ Scale photos to fill screen
☐ Automatic Ken Burns Effect
☐ Show titles
☐ Show my ratings
☐ Show slideshow controls

◉ Repeat music during slideshow
The music will repeat for as long as the slides play.

○ Fit slideshow to music
Slide durations will be adjusted to make the slides play for as long as the music plays.

Slideshow Format: [4:3 iDVD, TV ▼]

(Cancel) (OK)

Click OK to apply the changes.

making a slideshow

crop photos

Slideshows look best when your photos fill the screen. On the previous page, we chose a format of 4:3 iDVD, TV for our slideshow. Since most digital cameras create photos in 4:3 proportion—including the one used for this project—these will naturally fill a 4:3 screen. However, the vertically oriented pictures have a 3:4 proportion, and the empty space is filled in with ugly black bars. You can convert these to 4:3 by cropping them. Start by double-clicking the first vertical photo.

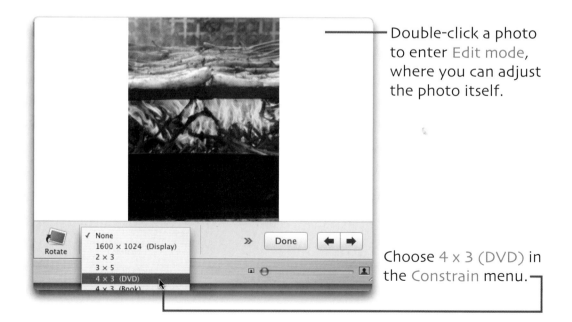

Double-click a photo to enter Edit mode, where you can adjust the photo itself.

Choose 4 x 3 (DVD) in the Constrain menu.

making a slideshow

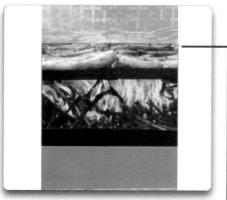 

Hold down the Option key to get a horizontal 4:3 box, and use the crosshair to select as large an area as possible from right to left.

Move the cursor within the selected area, and then move the selection box until it contains the desired part of the photo.

 When you're satisfied with the selection, click the Crop button at the bottom of the Edit mode screen.

The cropped portion of the photo is now displayed.

Click Done to save the changes. When you get back to Slideshow mode, you'll see the black bars have disappeared.

On your own: Crop the next photo (IMG_6035) to 4:3.

duplicate a photo

We're going to create a transition from a black and white copy of a photo to the original. To make the copy, make sure the first, newly cropped photo is selected, and choose Photos > Duplicate.

iPhoto File Edit Photos Share View Window Help

Get Info	⌘I
Batch Change...	⇧⌘B
Rotate Clockwise	⌘R
Rotate Counter Clockwise	⌥⌘R
My Rating	▶
Duplicate	⌘D
Delete From Album	⌘⌫
Revert to Original	

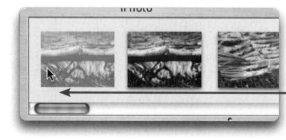

The copy is placed at the end of the slideshow (and the word copy is appended to its name in the Info window).

Drag the copy to the very beginning of the slideshow, in front of the original. The other photos will slide out of the way.

display in black/white

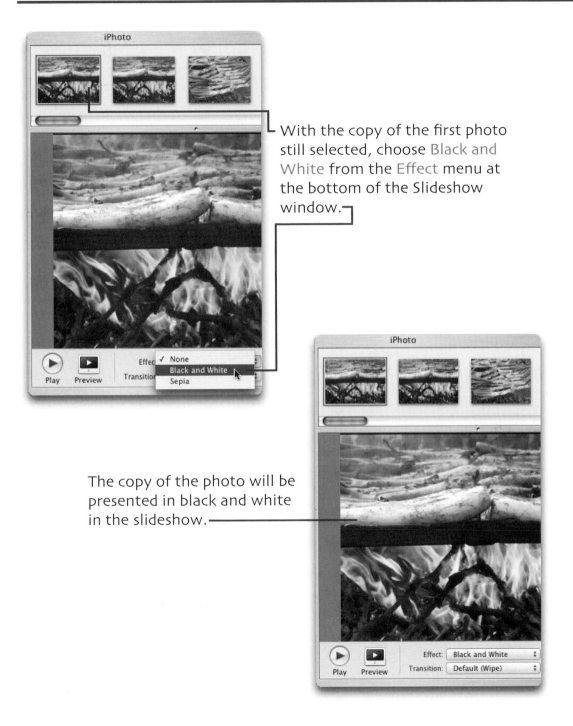

With the copy of the first photo still selected, choose Black and White from the Effect menu at the bottom of the Slideshow window.

The copy of the photo will be presented in black and white in the slideshow.

making a slideshow

adjust transition

Control-click the black and white slide in the middle of the Slideshow window and choose Adjust from the pop-up menu. (Or click the Adjust button.)

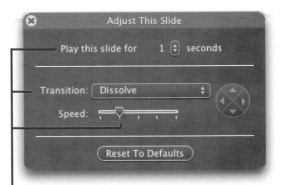

Then change the duration of this slide to 1 second, choose the Dissolve transition, and slow down the transition by moving the control to the left.

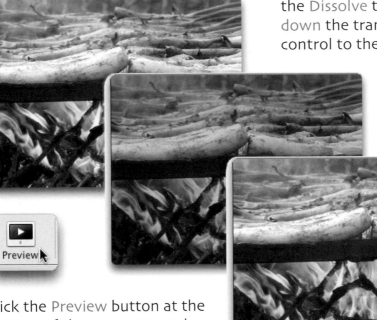

Click the Preview button at the bottom of the screen to see how the new transition will look.

making a slideshow

zoom in and center

The next photo (IMG_6503) has some extra details that are taking up too much of the picture.

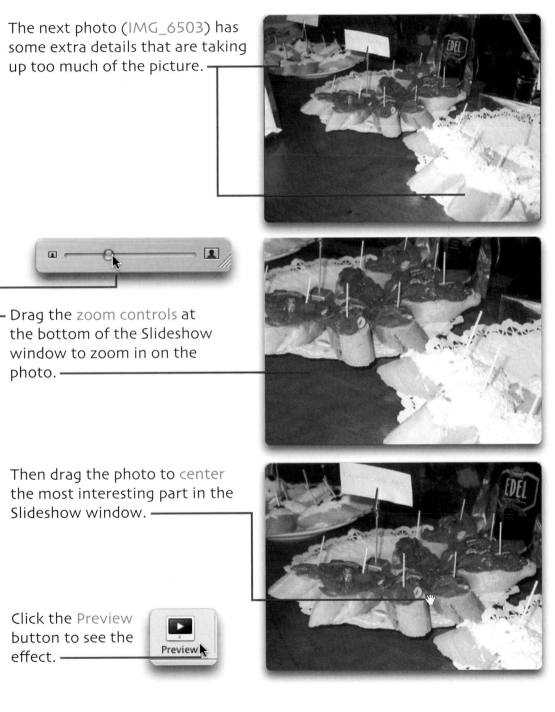

Drag the zoom controls at the bottom of the Slideshow window to zoom in on the photo.

Then drag the photo to center the most interesting part in the Slideshow window.

Click the Preview button to see the effect.

add motion to slides

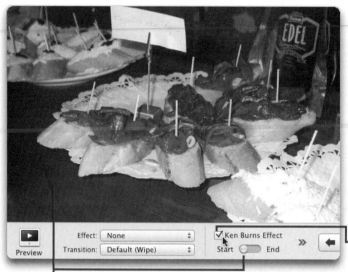

Film director Ken Burns (creator of the wildly successful Baseball and Civil War documentaries) popularized the technique of adding motion to still photos by zooming in on them and panning from one point to another. iPhoto lets you do this too. Start by checking Ken Burns Effect at the bottom of the Slideshow window.

iPhoto begins by showing you the initial zoom and position of the photo, indicated by the Start/End toggle on Start. This is where the camera will start, so to speak. Since we just got finished zooming in and centering the photo (on page 85) we don't need to adjust this further (but we could!).

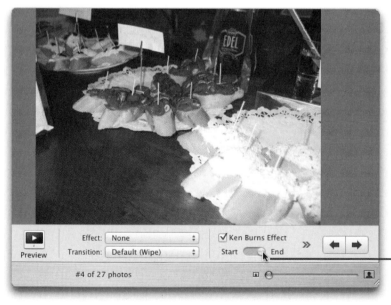

Click the Start/End toggle to switch it to End so that iPhoto shows you the current final zoom and position of the photo.

To change the final zoom and position, with the Start/End toggle on End, slide the zoom control over to the right to zoom in on the red pepper tapas. Drag the photo over slightly to center it. Then click Preview to see if you like it.

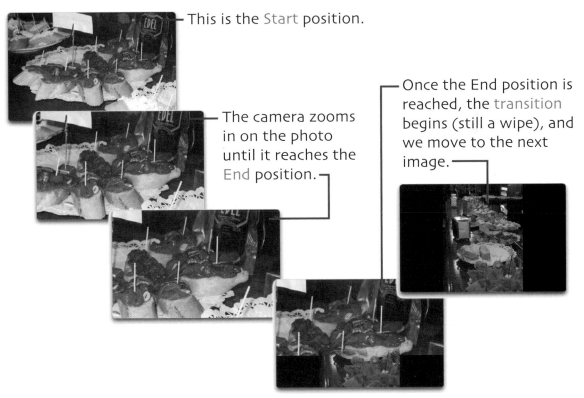

This is the Start position.

The camera zooms in on the photo until it reaches the End position.

Once the End position is reached, the transition begins (still a wipe), and we move to the next image.

making a slideshow

crop a photo into two

Cropping a vertical photo into a horizontal proportion loses half the photo. With this technique, we'll keep both halves. Start by selecting the fourth image (IMG_6506).

Choose Photos > Duplicate to create an independent copy of the selected photo as we did on page 82. You'll be able to crop the duplicate without affecting the original.

The copy is placed at the end of the slideshow (and the word copy is appended to its name in the Info window).

In the photo browser, drag the copy leftward until it directly follows the original.

making a slideshow

Double-click the original, select the bottom half of the photo in 4:3 proportion, click the Crop button, and then click Done. (See pages 80–81 for more details about cropping.)

Double-click the copy, select the top half of the photo in 4:3 proportion, click the Crop button, and then click Done.

You now have both halves of the original photo, and both will look good in the full screen. On the next page we'll pan from one half to the next.

pan from one half...

In this technique, we'll add motion to each of the two halves of the photo that we divided on the previous page, and then pan from one to the next. Start by selecting the first half (the bottom half).

Check the Ken Burns Effect, and then move the zoom slider over to the middle. Next, drag in the photo to center in on the ham and pickle tapas.

Switch the Start/End toggle to End and then reduce the zoom slightly. Then position the shot so that the red pepper tapas are just showing at the top of the screen.

Click the Adjust button and change the Transition to Push. Click the bottom arrow so that the next slide pushes this one away from top to bottom—and continues the movement of the pan.

...to the other half

Choose the second photo (the upper half of the original photo).

Check the Ken Burns Effect box.

This shot will push away the end shot of the first half, so zoom in and drag the bottom edge until it slightly overlaps the top edge of the first half (shown on the bottom of the previous page).

Finally, switch the Start/End toggle to End and pan out to see the entire array of incredible tapas by moving the zoom slider all the way to the left.

This one you have to preview on your own by clicking the Preview button. You'll start with a closeup of the ham and pickle tapas, panning out to a larger picture of the first half of the original photo, then pan (push) to the upper half which finally, pans out to reveal the whole bar.

making a slideshow

add and reorder photos

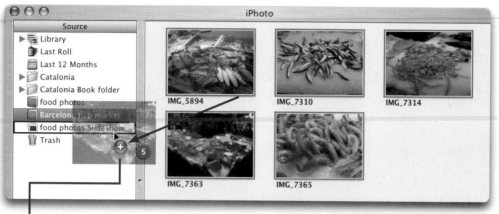

Add more photos to the slideshow by selecting the Barcelona fish market folder and then dragging the photos it contains to the food photos Slideshow in the Source list.

The newly added photos are placed at the very end of the slideshow.

Select all five photos in the photo browser and drag them to the spot just after the final tapas picture.

The photos are now in their new position.

add new transition

Select all five new fish photos (hold down the Shift key as you click the first photo, then click the last photo).

Then choose Droplet in the Transition menu at the bottom of the Slideshow window to apply the new transition to all five slides.

Click the Preview button to watch the drop of water change the first slide into the next.

auto enhance photos

If the colors are not quite right, double-click the photo (this one is IMG_7310) and then click the Enhance button at the bottom of the Edit mode window.

iPhoto adjusts the highlights and contrast automatically. (Choose Edit > Undo if you don't like the results.)

Click Done to return to the Slideshow window.

custom adjust photos

If the Enhance button doesn't do enough for you, or doesn't give you enough control, select the photo and click the Adjust button at the bottom of the Edit mode window.

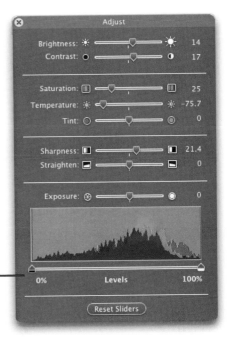

Use the Adjust panel to tweak the Brightness, Contrast, Saturation, Temperature, Tint, Sharpness, and Exposure. You can also straighten out a crooked photo by moving the control on the Straighten slider.

By upping the Brightness and Contrast, reducing the Saturation and Temperature, and gently increasing the Sharpness, I've made the fish look a lot colder. (Choose Edit > Undo if you don't like the results.)

Again, click Done to return to the Slideshow window.

change wipe direction

Using the same transition over and over can make your slideshow a little dull. For many (but not all) transitions, you can add interest by changing the direction that the transition progresses. Start by choosing the first photo in the next group (IMG_7316) and then click the Adjust button at the bottom of the Slideshow window.

In the Adjust This Slide box, choose Wipe from the Transition menu (see extra bits to learn why). Then click the right arrow to make the transition progress from left to right.

Choose the next slide (IMG_7370).

Again, choose Wipe from the Transition menu. This time, click the bottom arrow to make the transition progress from top to bottom.

Adjust This Slide

Play this slide for   3 ⬍   seconds

Transition: [Wipe   ⬍]

Speed: [━━━━●━━━━]

(Reset To Defaults)

Choose the third slide in the group (IMG_7305).

For the third slide in this group, choose Wipe and then click the left arrow to make the wipe progress from right to left.

Here's the transition from the first slide to the second. The second photo wipes out the first, starting at the left and moving toward the right.

In this transition, the third photo wipes out the second, starting at the top and moving toward the bottom.

Finally, the fourth photo wipes out the third, starting at the right and moving toward the left.

making a slideshow

add music

When you're ready to add background music to your slideshow, click the Music button at the bottom of the Slideshow window.

Make sure Play music during slideshow is checked at the top of the window. (It is by default.)

Song	Artist	Time
☑ Play music during slideshow		
▼ 🎵 Library		
🎵 Purchased Music		
❋ 50's and earlier		
❋ 60's Music		
❋ 70's Music		
❋ 80's Music		
❋ 90's Music		
❋ Catalan/Spanish smart		
🎵 Horse	Animal Sounds	0:06
🎵 Rooster	Animal Sounds	0:06
🎵 Rattlesnake	Animal Sounds	0:06
🎵 Goose	Animal Sounds	0:07
🎵 Cow	Animal Sounds	0:07
🎵 Donkey	Animal Sounds	0:07
🎵 Duck	Animal Sounds	0:07
🎵 Cat	Animal Sounds	0:07
🎵 Sheep	Animal Sounds	0:08
🎵 Monkey	Animal Sounds	0:08
🎵 Hyena	Animal Sounds	0:08
🎵 Frog	Animal Sounds	0:08

▶ 🔍 _____   4758 items

(Cancel)   (OK)

In the upper part of the window, you'll see your iTunes Library and the playlists it contains. Select the Library to display the songs it contains in the lower part of the window.

Click the Time column to put the songs in order of duration, so that you can easily find a song that matches the length of the slideshow.

making a slideshow

First, estimate the duration of the slideshow. We have 18 photos in our slideshow, with a duration of 3 seconds each, for a total of 54 seconds. Add 1 second for the one photo that lasts 4 seconds and then 1 second for each transition (for a total of 17). The total comes out at 1 minute, 12 seconds. Choose a song within a few seconds of that time.

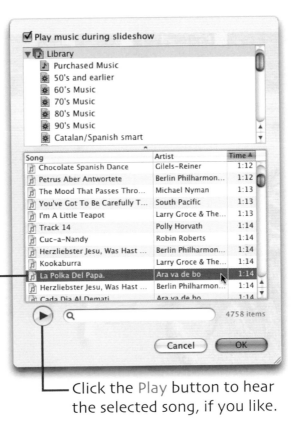

Click the Play button to hear the selected song, if you like.

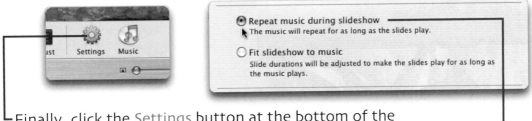

Finally, click the Settings button at the bottom of the Slideshow window. In the Settings box that appears, make sure Repeat music during slideshow is selected.

making a slideshow

play a slideshow

To view your slideshow on your screen (or on a screen connected to your computer, like a television or digital projector), first, select the slideshow in the Source list.

Make sure the first photo is selected in the photo browser at the top of the window.

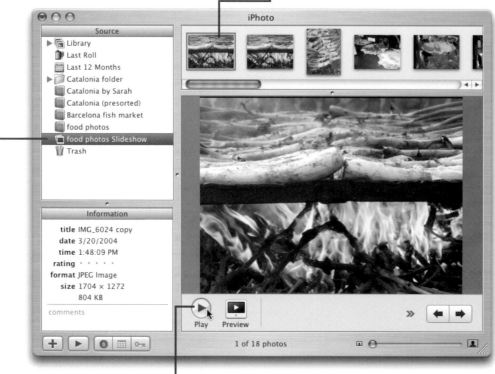

And then press the Play button to start the show.

making a slideshow

share a slideshow

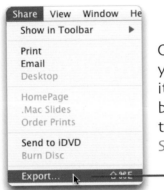

One of the easiest ways to share your slideshow is by exporting it into a QuickTime movie. Start by selecting your slideshow in the Source list and then choose Share > Export.

Choose a name for the QuickTime movie version of your slideshow and then choose a size. (To give you an idea, this slideshow takes up 6.3 Mb in Small size, 9 Mb at Medium size, and 28Mb in Large.) Click Export to create the movie.

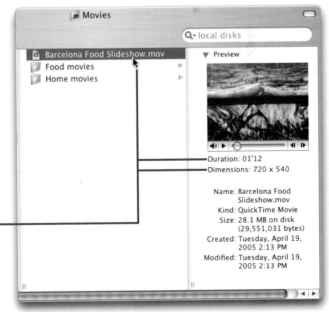

iPhoto saves the QuickTime version of your slideshow in your Movies folder, unless you specify otherwise. Select the movie in the Finder to see information about it, including its duration and size.

extra bits

put photos in order p. 75

- You can reorder your photos later on as well. See page 92.

create a slideshow p. 76

- If you don't see all the options at the bottom of the slideshow window, it's because your window isn't wide enough. In their place will be a double right arrow (>>) which, when you click on it, will reveal a pop-up menu with the remaining slideshow options.

- You can also select a bunch of photos and then click the Slideshow button to create a slideshow out of just those photos. The name of the slideshow still comes from the album containing the photos.

- Theoretically, you could be done already. You can watch your slideshow immediately by clicking the Play button. If you want to adjust your slideshow and play with the transitions and music, read on.

- You can reorder the photos in your slideshow at any time by dragging them into new positions in the photo browser at the top of the window.

adjust default settings p. 78

- You can apply the Ken Burns Effect to individual slides as described on pages 86–87.

- The duration, transition, and transition speed that you choose in the Settings box will be applied automatically to all the photos in your slideshow. It can be over-ridden by applying a different duration, transition, or transition speed to one or more photos with the Adjust This Slide box, as described on page 84.

- We'll discuss choosing music for a slideshow on pages 98–99.

- There are two principal formats or proportions for viewing pictures on a screen. The standard format is 4:3 and is still used by most televisions. This means that for every 4 inches across, you'll have three inches down. It's roughly equivalent to 1.34:1. Widescreen format has a proportion of 16:9 (or 1.78:1) and is close to the native format of most current movies, which are most often 1.85:1 or 2.35:1. The crucial bit is to choose a format that matches the proportion of your photos, or to crop your photos to match the proportion you've chosen (as described on pages 80–81).

- There are three options in the Settings box that we won't use in this project, but that are pretty self-explanatory: Show titles, Show my ratings, Show slideshow controls. The first displays the photo's title (or filename if you haven't given it a title) in the upper-left corner of the screen. If you check Show my ratings, the number of stars that you've given a photo (see page 11) will be displayed at the bottom of the photo. Finally, if you check Show slideshow controls, the play and pause buttons and other controls will always be visible (instead of only visible when you move the mouse).

crop photos p. 80

- You have to double-click the photo in the central Slideshow window, not the photo browser across the top of the window.

- You don't have to be in Slideshow view to crop a photo. You can double-click a photo from the main window or from a book to get to the Edit mode where the cropping tools are available.

- If you decide you don't like the way you cropped a photo, you can choose Undo right at the moment to go back. If you decide at some later date that you'd rather go back to the full picture, you can choose Photos > Revert to Original. Any changes you have made to the photo (including rotating, fixing red-eye, adjusting highlights, etc.) are removed.

- I find the way the 4:3 DVD option works rather strange. The first time you choose it, a large 3:4 rectangle appears in the middle of your photo. Choose it again, and the orientation changes to 4:3.

- When you edit a photo, the changes take effect everywhere you've used the photo, including any other slideshows or books you've already created or will create in the future. If you don't want to affect earlier uses of the photo, you can create a copy of the photo and change that. You'll go through that process in the next section (page 82).

- Slideshows intended to be shown in widescreen format should be cropped in a 16:9 proportion. You can choose Custom from the Constrain menu and then enter the desired proportion.

duplicate a photo p. 82

- When you duplicate a photo, iPhoto actually creates a new file for the photo, which acts completely independently of the original photo. You can crop it, change the lighting, add effects, or whatever, without affecting the original.

extra bits

display in black/white p. 83

- The black and white effect only applies to the photo in this slide-show. The photo will continue to be shown normally in the other slideshows or books that contain it, as well as in the main window.

- You can also create a sepia effect (a sort of old-fashioned, yellowed look) by choosing Sepia instead of Black and White in the Effect menu. Again, it only affects the slide in the current slideshow, not in other slideshows or books.

adjust transition p. 84

- We set the default duration, transition, and transition speed back on page 78. These will apply to all slides until and unless you change them as described here.

- You can select more than one photo at a time (in the slideshow's photo browser) and apply a new duration, transition, or transition speed to all of them at once.

- You can also get to the Adjust This Slide box by clicking the Adjust button at the bottom of the Slide-show window or, if the button is not visible, by choosing it from the >> menu at the bottom of the Slideshow window.

- You can leave the Adjust This Slide box open all the time, if you wish. Changes are applied as you make them and thus you don't have to close the box to apply the changes or to start working on other slides.

zoom in and center p. 85

- Zooming in on a photo, in contrast with cropping, does not affect it in any other slideshow or book.

add motion to slides p. 86

- The Start/End toggle simply shows you whether you're looking at the initial or the final position and zoom for the photo. So, if you want to see the initial position and zoom, click the Start/End toggle until Start is selected. If you want to change the initial position and zoom, click the Start/End toggle until Start is selected and then adjust the position and zoom. In the same way, if you want to see the final position, click the Start/End toggle until End is selected. If you want to change the final position and zoom, click the Start/End toggle until End is selected and then adjust the position and zoom.

- You can have iPhoto apply the Ken Burns Effect automatically to all of the photos in the slideshow by clicking the Settings button and checking Automatic Ken Burns Effect (which we turned off on page 79). You can still adjust the initial and final positions and zooms by hand, but you don't have to if you don't want to.

auto enhance photos p. 94

- You don't have to be in Slideshow view to enhance a photo. You can double-click a photo from the main window or from a book to get to the Edit mode where the enhancing tool is available.

custom adjust photos p. 95

- If you don't see the Adjust button, click the >> and choose Adjust from the pop-up menu.

- You don't have to be in Slideshow view to correct the colors in a photo. You can double-click a photo from the main window or from a book to get to the Edit mode where the color correction tools are available.

- You can always remove all your edits and return to the original photo by selecting the photo in the main window and choosing Photos > Revert to Original.

change wipe direction p. 96

- You must rechoose Wipe (without Default next to the name), or iPhoto won't apply the new direction. This is a bug. iPhoto wants to keep applying the default transition direction with the default transition. If you change the transition, (even choosing the same transition without the Default next to its name is enough), iPhoto will pay attention to the new transition direction.

- If you don't see the Adjust button, click the >> at the bottom of the Slideshow window and choose Adjust from the pop-up menu.

- The Adjust This Slide box can stay open as you go from slide to slide. You don't need to close it to apply changes.

- You can use the Adjust button to change the transition without changing the direction. (Or you can change the transition as we did on page 93.)

add music p. 98

- If you can't see the Music button, it's because your iPhoto window is too narrow. You can either make your window wider, or click the >> at the bottom of the Slideshow window and choose Music from the pop-up menu that appears.

extra bits

- You can also find a particular song by typing a few letters in the search box.

- If you want to choose more than one song, create a playlist on iTunes and then select that playlist in the music box.

- Although we've chosen Repeat music during slideshow, if you choose a song that is longer than the slideshow, the music won't have a chance to repeat.

- Choosing Fit music to slideshow causes iPhoto to change the duration of the slides to fit the music you choose. This seems like a great feature. You pick a song that you like and iPhoto makes your slideshow fit to it. Unfortunately, it doesn't work very well.

- You can find the exact duration of a slideshow by exporting it (choosing Share > Export) and then looking at it with the Quick-Time Player or in the Finder with previews visible (see page 101).

play a slideshow p. 100

- You can start a slideshow in the middle by choosing the photo with which you want to start before clicking the Play button.

- Pause a slideshow at any time by pressing the spacebar. Press the spacebar again to resume.

- Preview the effects and transition on a single slide by clicking the Preview button. Preview the effects and transitions of several slides by selecting those slides and clicking Play.

- There are more extra bits about slideshow controls on page 25.

- You can connect your computer to a TV or digital projector with an S-Video cable (assuming your Mac has an S-Video out jack, as most current models do). Then choose Displays in your System Preferences and click Detect Displays. Your computer screen should now be mirrored on the TV or projector. Click Play in iPhoto to start projecting your slideshow on the TV or projector.

share a slideshow p. 101

- You can burn the QuickTime movie directly to a CD or add it to a DVD.

- iDVD, Apple's DVD authoring software, come with iPhoto in the iLife package. It's a good tool for burning your iPhoto slideshows to DVD. You can have iPhoto export your movie in Large format, save it in the Movies folder, and then place it in your current iDVD project automatically by choosing Share > Send to iDVD.

appendix a:
photo book themes

I have a confession to make. I wrote this Appendix for myself. Every time I want to create a photo book, I have to try to remember which themes offer text mixed with photos, which have lots of photos on a page, which have the color scheme that I like the best—in short, which theme is best for my photos.

This Appendix takes the guesswork out of choosing a theme. You'll find information about each theme's page types, as well as the page designs that correspond to each type. Instead of creating complicated tables, I've opted to show you examples so you can get a feel for each theme and see exactly what you'll get.

I've also included the default layout pattern for each book theme. You can use the default layout pattern as a guide for choosing your photos (two for this page, one for that one, etc.), and then once the photos are in the proper order, click the Autoflow button to have iPhoto place all the photos on the appropriate pages for you. (See pages 60–61 for more about Autoflow.) However, don't forget that the default layout pattern is simply what iPhoto uses if you leave it all up to the program. You can, of course, change any of the page types or designs in your own book to suit your own photographs and your own taste.

picture book

The Picture Book theme fills its pages with photos, but not text. It offers blank, one-, two-, three-, four-, six-, eight-, and even sixteen-photo pages. The only place you'll find text is on the Introduction page and on the cover.

> Cover
> Introduction
> One
> ✓ Two
> Three
> Four
> Six
> Eight
> Sixteen
> Blank

A Picture Book starts with a one-photo cover with text, and an introduction on page 1.

Cover   Inside Cover   1

The default layout is extremely simple, though the flexibility of the layouts makes for almost infinite variations. The default layout starts on page 2 and goes: full, four, two, three.

2   3   4   5

Although each page type has only one page design, it varies widely depending on the orientation and order of the photos. Note how these two sets of pages have the exact same layout but look pretty different.

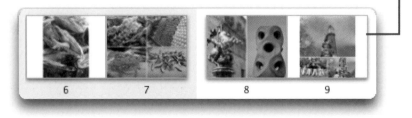

6   7   8   9

iPhoto makes it look like there's just one page design for one-photo pages.

But horizontally oriented photos completely fill a one-photo page...

...while vertically oriented photos have white bars on the right and left of the photo.

iPhoto offers just one design for two-photo pages, but by playing with the orientation and order of the photos, you can get four different layouts.

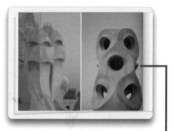

Two horizontal photos leave white bars across the top and bottom.

Two vertical photos fill the page.

Mixing one vertical with one horizontal photo, in either order, leaves smaller horizontal bars.

photo book themes

picture book (cont).

iPhoto's three-photo page type also has only one design to choose from in the menu.

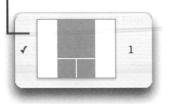

But certainly, three horizontal photos look different from...

...three vertical ones.

Notice what happens when you mix one vertical photo with two horizontal ones. This time it's the order of the photos that changes the page design.

When you mix one horizontal photo with two vertical ones, you also have three different choices of page layouts, depending on how you order the photos.

photo book themes

The more photos we add, the more possibilities there are. iPhoto's sole four-photo page design can be used in countless ways (actually 16).

With four horizontal photos, you fill the page completely.

With four vertical photos, you get wide, white margins on both sides.

Here are one of each orientation on each line, and in opposite corners. You could just as easily switch the corners, or group one type on the right, or on the left.

The same two verticals and two horizontals leave wider margins when grouped horizontally. You can also put the verticals above and the horizontals below.

In these designs, there's one of one kind and three of the other. You can move the oddball to any of the four corners, making four separate designs with each combination.

I like it when they fill the whole page (3 horizontals and one vertical).

photo book themes

picture book (cont).

Instead of changing and adapting the design to suit the
orientation of the photos, the Picture Book's six-photo
page designs crop and cram the photos as necessary into
rigid, immutable frames...

...which can make for
rather disastrous layouts
if you're not careful.

Here are page designs 2 and 3 with the same 6 photos (5 horizontal,
1 vertical). What you achieved earlier by changing the order of the
photos, now requires choosing a different page design.

These are designs 4
(left) and 6, with the
same four verticals
and two horizontals.

The eight-photo page design in the Picture Book theme works much like the six- and sixteen-photo pages: the frames are fixed and photos are cropped to fit. Choose them carefully.

The sixteen-photo page is a cacophony of small, horizontal photos. You can use vertical shots, but they'll be cropped mercilessly, unless you tell iPhoto not to. Double-click to pan as needed (see page 48).

photo book themes

travel

The Travel book theme is characterized by tilted photos, many varied page designs, and passport stamps right on the backgrounds. It offers blank, one-, two-, three-, four-, six-, and seven-photo pages, with little text.

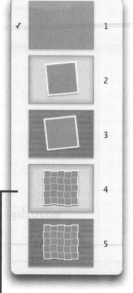

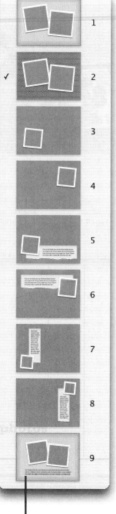

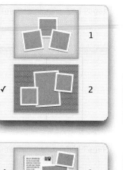

The four-photo page is particularly unique and includes a postcard and slip of paper that you can add text to.

In general terms, the Travel theme offers tilted photos on passport-like stamped cream or orange backgrounds. The variations are so numerous I felt compelled to show you all of them (except the blank pages, see the extra bits).

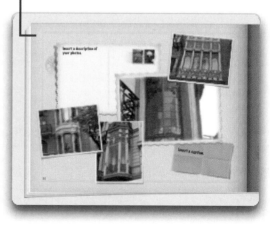

There are some lovely two-photo combinations, none of which are included in the default layout (but see page 63 for an example).

The Travel book theme has a two-photo cover with two types of text. The Introduction on page 1 also has two text areas. Page 2 is a cream (2) photo page.

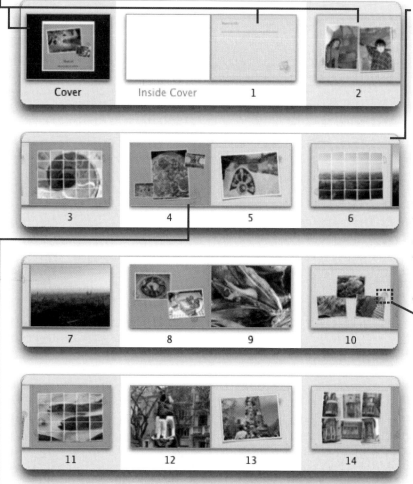

The default layout for Travel theme books starts on page 3 and goes: orange mosaic, orange (3), cream, cream mosaic, full, orange (2), cream, cream (3), orange mosaic, full, cream, cream (6) and then repeats. On alternating repeats, the last page design is cream (2) instead of cream (6).

The passport stamps come in various preset languages.

The first orange (3) is a special design. The central photo looks as if it got folded up in the tourist's pocket. You must place the central, vertically oriented photo first, or the design reverts to a regular orange (3) design. The layout is not repeated and cannot be chosen from the menu (see page 52 for an example).

photo book themes

watercolor

The Watercolor theme is characterized by textured, pastel-colored paper and fancy, elegant fonts. It offers blank, one-, two-, three-, four-, and six-photo pages.

Cover
Introduction
✓ One
Two
Three
Four
Six
Blank

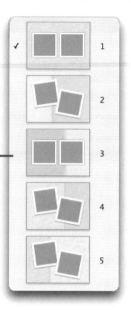

Each page type offers a straight photo on a blue plain or blue bicolor background or a skewed photo on one of three bicolor backgrounds.

In addition, the one-photo page offers a full design, 5 different colored mosaic designs, and three bicolor designs with text.

Note that some of the backgrounds have the darker part on the inside edge, some have it on the outside edge.

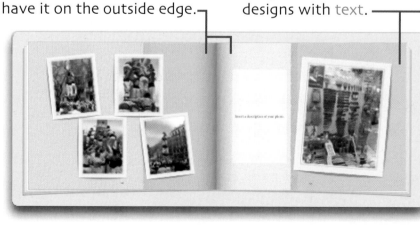

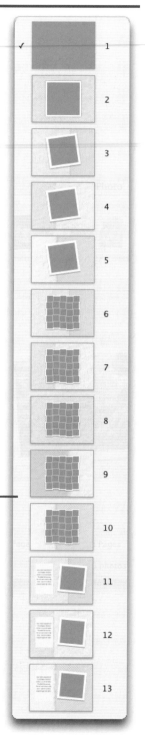

The Watercolor theme has no photo on the cover. It uses a fancy, cursive style font and has three text areas. The introduction on page 1 has two text areas.

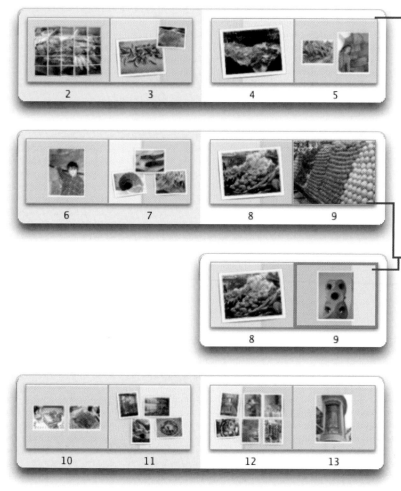

The default layout pattern is blue mosaic, bicolor green (2), bicolor orange, straight blue (2), straight blue, bicolor purple (3), bicolor green, full, straight blue (2), bicolor orange (4), bicolor purple (6), straight blue.

The full page is a special one. If you place a vertically oriented photo there (or one lands there after you choose Autoflow), you'll get a straight, bicolor blue, one-photo page, which you won't find in any menu.

contemporary

The Contemporary book theme has bold, simple designs with text on all pages except full-photo pages. There are blank, one-, two-, and three-photo page types.

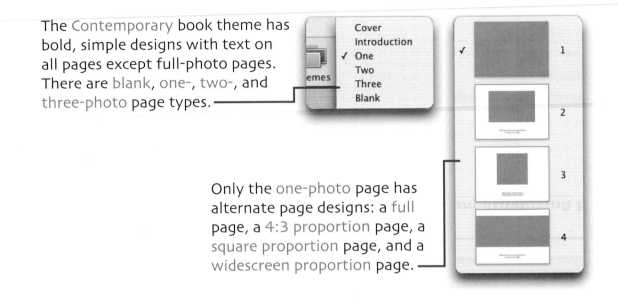

Only the one-photo page has alternate page designs: a full page, a 4:3 proportion page, a square proportion page, and a widescreen proportion page.

Double-click a square layout to reveal the zoom control and center the image as described on page 48.

The square and widescreen one-photo page designs work well together since they have the same height. I don't know why they didn't include the gorgeous widescreen design in the default layout.

The Contemporary theme
has one photo on the cover
that can be either vertical (as
shown here) or horizontal. The
introduction (page 1) has two
text areas.

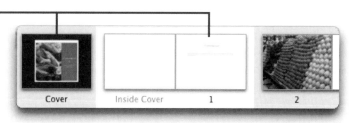

The default layout pattern
goes one 4:3, two, full,
full, one square, three,
full, full, full, full.

The pattern begins to repeat on page 13 (same as
page 3). It looks like a square, but it's actually a 4:3
proportion page with a vertically oriented photo. This
is the least successful of the designs, in my opinion,
mostly because it doesn't line up with the other designs.

Mixing photos
of different
orientations
can create an
interesting effect
on a three-photo
page.

folio

The Folio book theme is characterized by large photos on either black or white backgrounds and captions on every page. There are one- and two-photo pages as well as four different text page options.

| Cover |
| Title Page |
| ✓ Text Page |
| About Page |
| Contact Page |
| One |
| Two |
| Blank |

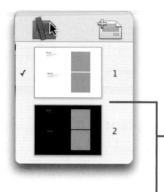

Each page type has two otherwise identical page designs: one with a white background and one with a black background.

The appearance of Folio pages depends considerably on the orientation of the photos. This spread has the same page types and designs as the one directly above it, but the orientation of the photos makes it look quite different.

The Folio theme's cover has a single photo and text. Page 1 is a Title Page. Page 2 is a Black Full.

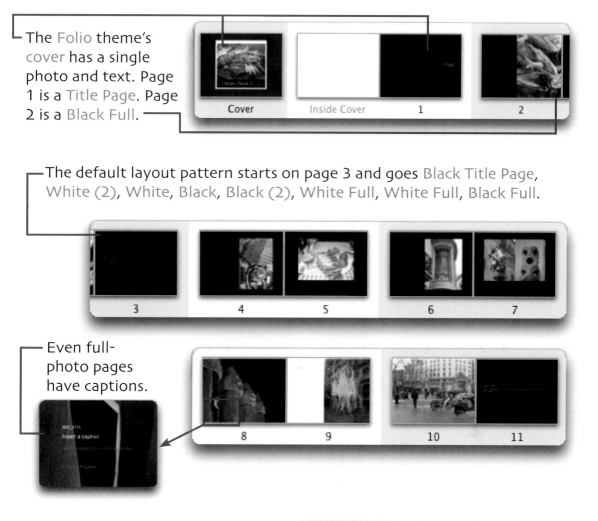

The default layout pattern starts on page 3 and goes Black Title Page, White (2), White, Black, Black (2), White Full, White Full, Black Full.

Even full-photo pages have captions.

The default Folio layout ends with two text pages: the About Page on page 19 and the Contact Page on page 20.

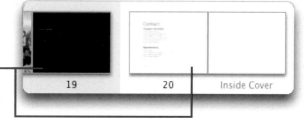

photo book themes

crayon

The Crayon theme uses six different textured, colored backgrounds to display blank, one-, two-, three-, four-, and six-photo pages.

Each page type offers a straight layout on a white background or skewed photos on one of five colored backgrounds. The two-photo page type also offers a page design with text.

Notice how the outline color changes depending on the photo's orientation.

The orientation doesn't affect the layout much otherwise.

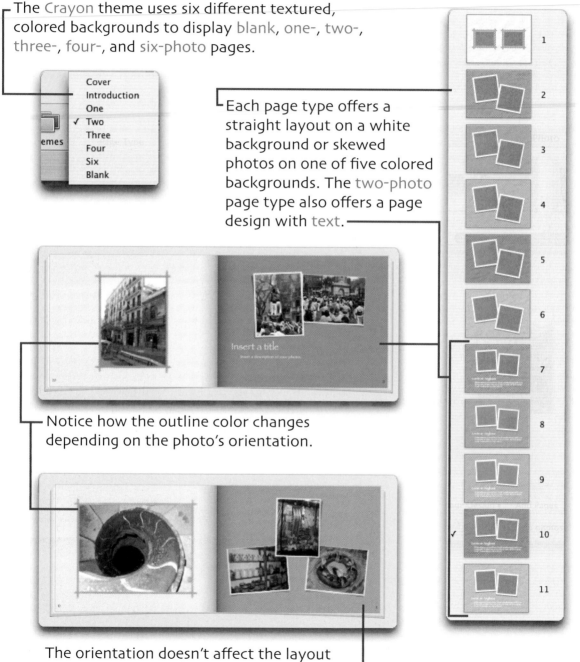

The Crayon theme has a one-photo cover with text. The introduction page (page 1) has two text areas on a green background.

| Cover | Inside Cover | 1 |

The default layout pattern for the Crayon theme is basically color background, two straight (S) pages, color background, and then repeat. To be more precise, it is:

purple (2), S, S(2), orange, pink (4), S, S (2), full, blue (3), S, S, green (6), purple, S, S (2), orange, pink (2), S, S, full, blue (3), S, S, green (6). (If no number is indicated, it's a one-photo page.)

Why isn't page 21 a full? Because iPhoto starts the pattern over after the initial final page 20.

photo book themes

baby boy or girl

The Baby Boy and Baby Girl themes are identical, except for their rather stereotypical colors: pastel blue and pink. They feature blank, one-, two-, three-, four-, and six-photo pages, along with two special text pages, one for information about the baby and one for stories.

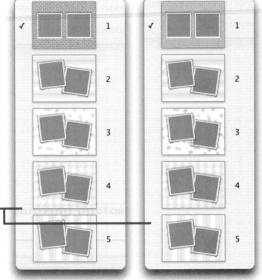

All the photo pages— and the information page—offer a choice of five patterned backgrounds: brick, horizontal stripes, confetti, checks, and vertical stripes. (Straight photos are only available on a brick background.)

One-photo pages can also be filled with the photo or be broken into mosaics, though I don't quite see the point of the latter, especially with baby pictures.

iPhoto will crop the photo on the story page (inexplicably called Introduction) if necessary to fit the vertical frame. Double-click to reveal the zoom control and then drag in the frame to center.

The Baby themes have one photo and text on the cover. There is a special information page, with a photo, where you can list the baby's name, weight, birth date, etc.

The default layout for the Baby theme is one, brick (2), one, multiple stripes, and then repeat with minor variations (descriptions without numbers are one-photo pages):
confetti, brick (2), full, vertical stripes (4), checks, brick (2), brick, horizontal stripes (2), confetti mosaic, story page, full, v-stripes (3), checks, brick, brick, horizontal stripes (6), confetti, brick (2), brick, vertical stripes (2), checks, brick (2), brick, horizontal stripes (3).

What looks like plain blue (or pink) on screen is actually the brick pattern.

classic

Classic is one of iPhoto's old themes. The layouts are simple and clear with titles and captions underneath each photo. It offers blank, one-, two-, three-, four-, and six-photo pages.

The Classic theme's page designs adapt to the photos' orientation.

Up to level 2
The Barcelona team constructs a 7 story three person tower.

Every photo gets one text area for the title and another for a description.

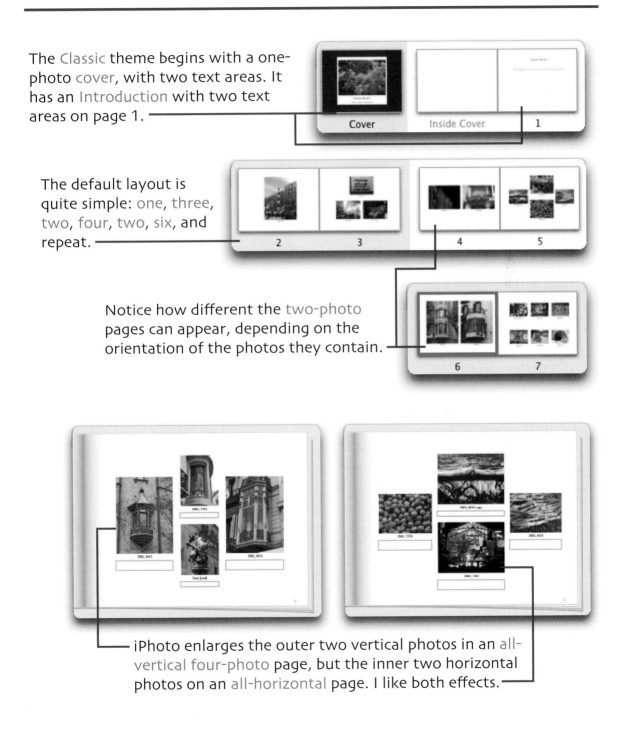

The Classic theme begins with a one-photo cover, with two text areas. It has an Introduction with two text areas on page 1.

The default layout is quite simple: one, three, two, four, two, six, and repeat.

Notice how different the two-photo pages can appear, depending on the orientation of the photos they contain.

iPhoto enlarges the outer two vertical photos in an all-vertical four-photo page, but the inner two horizontal photos on an all-horizontal page. I like both effects.

photo book themes

story book

The Story Book theme is characterized by wildly slanted images and big blocks of informal text. It offers blank, one-, two-, and three-photo pages, an introduction, and a special End page that combines three photos with text.

Cover
Introduction
One
✓ Two
Three
End
Blank

All four of these pages have the same two-photo page design—but the orientations of the photos they contain makes them completely different.

When you mix one horizontal and one vertical photo on a two-photo page, their order determines whether they are displayed vertically (as on the left) or horizontally. Simply exchange the photos if you want to get the other layout.

photo book themes

The Story Book theme begins with a one-photo cover with two text areas. The introduction has room for a title, three photos, and text.

Cover · Inside Cover · 1

Like all of the old themes, Story Book has a very simple repeat: one, two, three, two. Thanks to the variation in orientation, however, these two sets of four pages look pretty different.

2 · 3 · 4 · 5

6 · 7 · 8 · 9

The End

And they all lived squarely ever after.

At first glance, the End page looks like a glorified three-photo page with pre-entered text. In fact, it has rigid, square frames into which iPhoto automatically fits your 4:3 photos.

If you'd rather the photos be square, Control-click the photos and uncheck Fit Photo to Frame Size. (And you can edit the text as much as you like.)

collage

The Collage theme is characterized by square frames. You can either crop your photos to the proper proportion or have iPhoto do it for you. Or you can use regular 4:3 proportioned photos and leave extra space. There are blank, one-, two-, three-, four-, and six-photo pages, as well as an Introduction page and a special one-photo page with text off to the side.

The Collage theme begins with a 4:3 photo on the cover and an introduction that contains both a square photo and text.

The default layout goes two, introduction, four, one, three, six, one with text. I've let iPhoto crop all the photos into a square shape for me, as described in more detail on the following page.

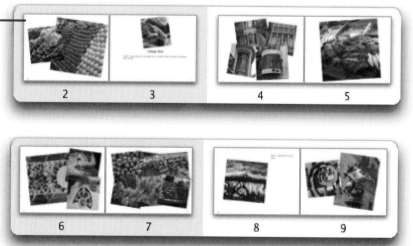

Here are the three-
and six-photo pages
with standard 4:3
photos. They look
all right.

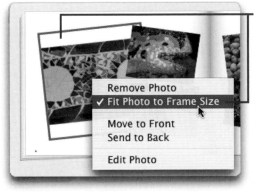

To let iPhoto crop the photos to the proper
proportion, Control-click the first photo and
uncheck Fit Photo to Frame Size.

The photo fills the
square frame. Now
double-click the
photo and drag it
to show the part
you like best. ——

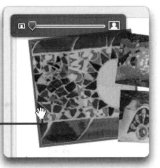

When you're done squaring up all the photos,
they look a lot more impressive.

photo book themes

portfolio

The Portfolio theme has two text areas per photo like the Classic book but uses flexible photo frames like Picture Book. It offers blank, one-, two-, three-, and four-photo pages and an Introduction text page.

Portfolio starts with a one-photo cover and two text areas. Page 1 is an introduction made up of two text areas.

The default layout pattern goes: one, three, one, four, one, two.

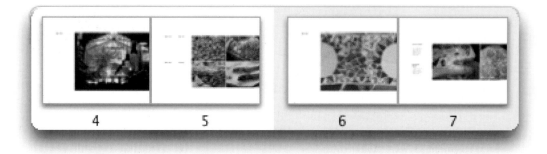

photo book themes

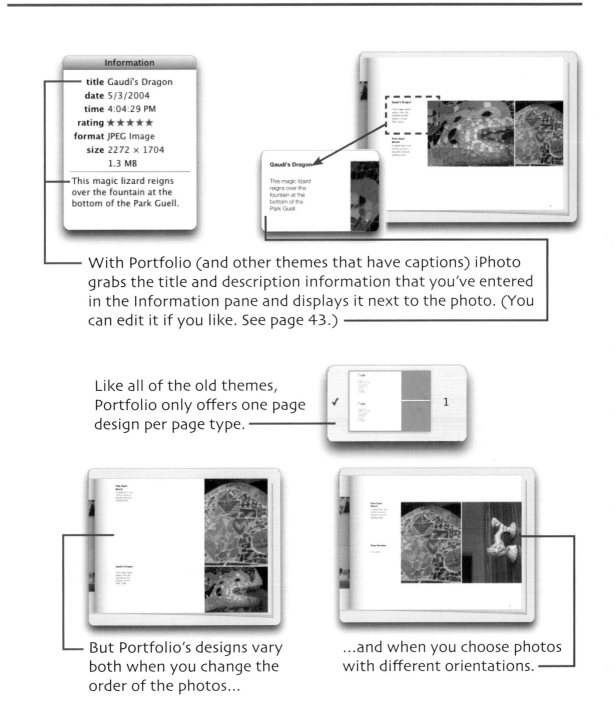

With Portfolio (and other themes that have captions) iPhoto grabs the title and description information that you've entered in the Information pane and displays it next to the photo. (You can edit it if you like. See page 43.)

Like all of the old themes, Portfolio only offers one page design per page type.

But Portfolio's designs vary both when you change the order of the photos...

...and when you choose photos with different orientations.

photo book themes

year book

The Year Book theme has the distinction of having the largest number of photos on a single page: 32! It also offers blank, one-, two-, four-, six-, eight-, twelve-, eighteen-, and twenty-photo pages, and an introduction.

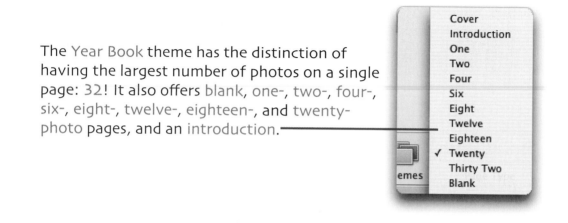

The Year Book theme has a one-photo cover and standard introduction page, each with two text areas. It starts with a one-photo and then a two-photo page.

| Cover | Inside Cover | 1 | 2 | 3 |

| 4 | 5 | 6 | 7 | 8 | 9 |

The default layout pattern is one, two, six, six, twelve, twenty, and then repeat. It's clearly designed to give you an idea of what's available, more than to be a real layout that you'd want to use for your year book.

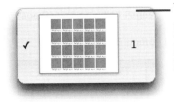

Year Book has only one page design for each page type. While the one- and two-photo page designs adapt to both vertical and horizontal photos, the other page types are best suited for a specific orientation.

The four-photo page has square frames.——

The six-, twelve-, and twenty-photo pages have horizontal frames.——

The eight-, eighteen-, and thirty-two-photo pages have vertical frames.——

catalog

The Catalog theme has a simple design, using mostly square frames. It offers blank, one-, four-, and eight-photo pages, as well as an introduction page.

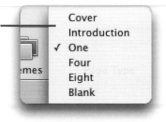

 Each page type has a single page design with two text areas to the upper-right of each photo which are automatically filled from the photo's information pane.

The Catalog has a standard one-photo cover and introduction page, each with two text areas.

The default layout, like that of Year Book, is more to give you an idea of the layouts available rather than for using as the basis for a real book. The pattern goes one, one, four, four, eight, eight, and repeat. Whee.

The one-photo page varies slightly according to the photo's orientation.

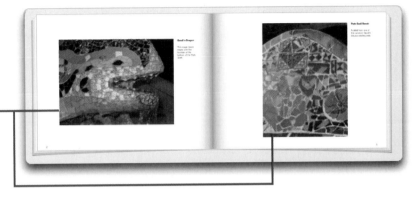

The four- and eight-photo pages use square frames. As long as the Fit Photo to Frame Size option is not checked, iPhoto will fill the squares with your photos.

Here is the same page with iPhoto shoehorning (they call it "fitting") each standard 4:3 photo into the square frame and leaving white space on the edges.

Note that all the photographs are aligned to the top-right corner of the square frame.

extra bits

picture book p. 108

- With the six-, eight-, and sixteen-photo page designs, iPhoto crops the photos by default, but you can tell it not to by Control-clicking the photo and checking Fit Photo to Frame Size. I don't think it looks that great this way, though. You can find more details about this command in the Collage theme tips on pages 139–140.

travel p. 114

- The Travel theme has three different colored blank pages—white, cream, and orange—that I just didn't have room to show you.

- The passport stamps can be placed on top of the photo by Control-clicking the photo and choosing Send to Back.

watercolor p. 116

- The Watercolor theme offers various different colored blank pages. It bugs me that you can't make the dark areas (or light areas for that matter) match up across a two-page spread.

- The order of the page designs for two-photo pages is a little weird. It should be plain blue, bicolor blue, and then tilted green, tilted purple, and tilted orange, in that order, just as they are for (most of) the other page types.

- For that matter, the one-photo page design menu is off too. The straight blue bicolor is missing altogether (though it shows up in the default layout), and the rest of the designs are only vaguely grouped together and ordered properly.

contemporary p. 118

- iPhoto automatically crops your photos to fit the square or widescreen frames. You can have iPhoto leave the proportion of your photos alone by Control-clicking a photo and checking the Fit Photo to Frame Size option. See the Collage theme tips on pages 139–140 for more details.

folio p. 120

- Text is automatically entered into the text boxes from the photo's information pane—if there's anything there (see page 10 for more about labeling your photos).

- You can also add text directly in Book view. It will override any text that came from the information pane. The strange thing is that if you rearrange the photos on the page, the directly-typed text box stays put and overrides the information from any new photos that you put there. Weird.

extra bits

- The text box border goes away once you add some text.

- If you don't want iPhoto to automatically fill your text boxes with the data in the information pane, click the Settings button at the bottom of the Book window and then deselect Automatically enter photo information in the box that appears.

- I don't recommend changing fonts with the Settings box described in the preceding tip. I think it's buggy (at least up to version 5.0.2.) Consult my web site for updates (see page xiii).

- These tips apply to all of the photo book themes with text boxes for titles and captions (Folio, Classic, Portfolio, Year Book, and Catalog).

crayon p. 122

- The Crayon theme offers six different blank pages: one of each color to match the other page designs, plus white.

classic p. 126

- The same tips from the Folio theme apply to Classic (see pages 138–139).

story book p. 128

- The End page design uses square frames, not the standard 4:3 (or 3:4) used elsewhere. By default, iPhoto will reduce your 4:3 photos to fit, leaving empty white bars in its wake. The horizontal pictures look OK because they overlap. Square pictures look even better. See the Collage theme (page 130 and the next tip section) for more details on filling square frames.

collage p. 130

- Cropping your photos this way does not affect their appearance in any other book or slideshow. Of course, you can crop your photos yourself with the Crop button (see pages 80–81), but then they will be cropped everywhere, not just in this particular book project.

- I find the wording of the Fit Photo to Frame Size command extremely confusing. Does it mean shoehorn the photo inside the frame without changing its proportions? Or does it mean make the photo fill the frame? It actually means the former. With this command checked, iPhoto will reduce the size of your photo, while maintaining its proportions, in order to fit it inside the frame. It's a bit like watching a widescreen movie on a

extra bits

standard 4:3 television set. When you uncheck the option, iPhoto lops off the sides of the photo (or the top and bottom if it's a vertically oriented photo), and fills the frame. Which is basically what happens when they "adapt" movies to show on television.

- At any rate, in order to fill the frames with your 4:3 photos, you don't want iPhoto to Fit Photo to Frame Size and thus there should be no checkmark next to the command. The worst part is that you have to choose the command when it has a checkmark next to it in order to make the checkmark disappear. Ugh!

portfolio p. 132
- The same tips from the Folio theme apply to Portfolio (see pages 138–139).

year book p. 134
- For more details on taking advantage of the four-photo page's square frames, see the Collage theme on page 130.
- The same tips from the Folio theme apply to Year Book (see pages 138–139).

catalog p. 136
- The same tips from the Folio theme apply to Catalog (see pages 138–139).

index

Symbols

>> (double right arrow), menu
  51, 70, 102
4:3 proportion 79, 80, 102
  photos 131–132, 137

A

adding pages to book 71
adding photos
  to book 62
  to slideshow 92
Add Page command 71
Add to Library command 23
Adjust button 95
albums
  can't drag photo to from trash
   26
  creating 12–14
   by dragging 14
  deleting 27
  information about 27
  removing photos from 13
  smart albums, creating 32–33
  storing in folders 15
  viewing number of photos
   in 27
  vs Library 27
Align photos to grid option 24
Apple Account 67, 72
arrows for navigating 44, 77
arrow keys
  for navigating photo books
   68
aspect ratio. See format
Autoflow command 60–61
  and default layout patterns
   107
  and photo browser 61, 70
  placement order 70
  revealing button when hidden
   70

Automatically enter photo
  information, option 140
automatic captions 26, 133,
  136, 138, 139, 140
automatic grid, turning off 24

B

Baby Boy/Girl book theme
  124–125
bad photos, removing 8
black and white, displaying
  photos in 83
Black and White command 83
black bar, and sorting manually
  35, 75
black bars, and slideshow format
  80
blank pages, colored
  in Crayon theme 138
  in Travel theme 138
  in Watercolor theme 138
blowing up photos. See enlarging
  photos
blue album icon 12–13
blue ball
  for magnifying/reducing view
   5, 42, 75
  for zooming in on slide 85
blue dot
  and date searches 20
  and keyword searches 19
blue keywords 29
blue key icon 19
book. See photo books
Book button 36–37
book icon 38
Book mode 38
brightness, adjusting 95
burning slideshows to DVD 106
Burns, Ken. See Ken Burns Effect

C

calendar icon 20. See also dates
camera, importing photos from
  2
Catalog book theme 136–137
CD
  exporting slideshow to 106
  importing from 3
centering photos
  in books 48, 54–55
  in slideshows 85, 90–91
checkmark keyword 28
Classic book theme 126–127
Clean Up Book command 70
Collage book theme 130–131
comments
  adding 10
  uses for 26
Constrain menu 80
Contemporary book theme
  118–119
contrast, adjusting 95
  automatically 94
cost of photo book 36
cover of photo book 40–41
Crayon book theme 122–123
creased photo design 69
Create Film Roll command 23
cropping photos
  for books 113, 124, 131,
   138, 139
  for slideshows 80–81, 88–89,
   103
Crop button 81, 89, 139

index

D

date
  changing in information pane 26
  finding all photos from particular 29
  of film rolls 24
  searching by 20
    tips 29
  sorting photos by 30
default layout pattern
  explanation of 107
  for Baby Boy/Girl 125
  for Catalog 136
  for Classic 127
  for Collage 130
  for Contemporary 119
  for Crayon 123
  for Folio 121
  for Picture Book 108
  for Portfolio 132
  for Story Book 129
  for Travel 115
  for Watercolor 117
  for Year Book 134
deleting albums 27
deleting photos
  from albums 13
  from book 70
  from camera 2
  from Library 8
  getting them back 9
  permanently 9
description, viewing 4
Description field, for film rolls 2
digital camera, importing photos from 2
direction of transition. See transition direction
Dissolve transition 84
dot. See blue dot
Double-sided pages option 37
double right arrow (>>) menu 51, 70, 102

dragging photos
  from one album to another 27
  from Trash 26
  to album 13
  to book 62
  to center them 54
  to change page design 56–57
  to create album 14, 27
  to import 3
  to place them 40
Droplet transition 93
Duplicate command 82, 88
duplicating photos 82, 88
duration of slides 7, 84
duration of slideshow 101
DVD
  exporting slideshow for 106
  importing from 3

E

editing text 43, 138, 139, 140
  yellow warning triangle 68
Edit mode
  auto enhancing photos 94
  cropping photos 80
  custom adjusting photos 95
  entering from Book mode 69
  entering from Slideshow mode 94, 95
  entering with Edit Photo command 46
  fixing red eye 46–47
  leaving 24
Edit Photo command 46
Effect menu 83
email, importing photos from 23
Empty Trash command 9, 26
Enhance button 94
enhancing photos 94
enlarging photos 48, 54–55
  in slideshows 85, 91
example files, for this book xiii
Export command 101
exposure, adjusting 95

extra bits
  description xii
  for importing and organizing 23–30
  for photo books 68–72
  for photo book themes 138–140

F

facing layouts, viewing 49. See also spreads
Ferry, Ken (and Keyword Assistant) 28
file names, and photo titles 26
film rolls
  and Library 24
  create new 23
  date of 24
  hiding/revealing photos in 24
  importing photos 3
  move photos between 23
  not visible 24
  order of 24
  sorting 4
  triangle, leading 4
  viewing 4
Fit music to slideshow option 106
Fit Photo to Frame Size command 68, 129, 131, 137, 138, 139
fixing red eye 46–47
folders
  conflicting names 68
  creating 15
  hiding/revealing contents 68
  nesting 28
  order in Source list 28
  organizing book files in 39
Folio book theme 120–121
fonts 43
  and Setting button 68
format, slideshow
  choosing 79
  cropping for 80–81, 103

frames, photo
    description 38
    dragging photos to 40–41,
        52–53
    filling with Autoflow 60–61
    indicating page design 45
    orientation of 41
    removing photos from 59
    square 129, 130–131, 137,
        138, 139
    widescreen 138

G

Gaudí, Antoni (architect of La
    Pedrera) 63

H

highlights, adjust automatically
    94
horizontal photos.
    See orientation of photos
how this book works x–xii

I

images. See photos
Image Capture program 23
importing photos
    by dragging 3, 74
    creating album
        simultaneously 23, 74
    from a disk or folder 3, 74
    from camera 2
    from email 23
    from scanner 23
    individual photos 23
    labeling 2
Information button 4, 10
information pane 4, 10, 138,
    139, 140
    keyboard shortcuts 26
introduction page 45
iPhoto discussion board 72

K

Ken Burns Effect
    applying 86–87, 90–91,
        104–105
    turning off 79
key, blue (icon) 19
keywords
    applying 18
    checkmark 28
    defining 16–17
    keyboard shortcuts 28
    order of 28
    removing 17, 28
    renaming 17, 28
    searching by 19
        tips 29
    viewing 18
Keywords command 18
Keywords icon 16
Keyword Assistant 28

L

landscape-oriented photos 6
Last 12 Months (Library subset)
    15, 27
Last Roll (Library subset) 15, 27
length of photo book 71
levels, adjusting 95
Library
    and film rolls 24
    deleting photos from 8
    importing photos to 3
    restoring photos 9
    viewing film rolls 4
    vs albums 27

M

Macintosh selection shortcuts
    25
magnifying the view 5, 42, 46,
    47
    to optimum size 24
Move to Front command 58

Move to Trash command 8
music, adding to slideshow
    98–99
Music button 98–99
    hiding/revealing 105
My Rating command 11

N

navigating
    in photo book 44, 68
    through slideshows 25, 106
    through slideshow photos 77
New Album command 12–13
New Album From Selection
    command 27, 34
New Folder command 15

O

ordering book 66–67
    tips 72
organizing photos 1–30
    deleting 8
    emptying trash 9
    film rolls 4
    importing 2–3
    keywords 16–17
    labeling photos 10
    rating photos 11
    reviewing 7
    rotating 6
    searching for 19–21
    viewing size 5
    with albums 12–14
    with folders 15
orientation of photos 41,
    108–113, 112, 115, 117,
    119, 120, 122, 126, 128,
    133, 135, 137
overlapping photos in photo
    book 58

index

P

pages
  adding to book 71
  number of 71
  removing from book 65
  reordering in book 64
    individual 71
page designs. See also Appendix A
  changing 50–51, 61, 63
  changing by dragging 56–57
  rearranging photos and 69
  special 52, 69
Page Design menu 50–51
page numbering and reordering 64
page types 45, 63. See also Appendix A
  and photo browser 68
Page Type menu 45
page view icon 44, 64
panning photos
  in book 48, 54–55
  in slideshow 86–87, 91
panorama, create 54–55
passport stamps 115, 138
  moving in front of photo 69
pausing slideshow 106
PDF file of photo book 72
Pedrera (building) 63
performance, improving 24
photos
  adding motion to in slideshow 86–87
  adding to book 62
  adding to slideshow 92
  adjusting 95
  albums of 13–14
  autoflowing 60
  auto enhancing 94
  brightness, adjusting 95
  centering 54–55, 85
  comments, adding 10
  contrast, adjusting 94, 95

cropping
  for books 113, 124, 131, 138, 139
  for slideshows 80–81, 88–89
deleting 26
dragging individual 23
duplicating 82
enlarging 48, 54–55, 85, 90–91
example files for this book xiii
exposure, adjusting 95
fixing red eye 46–47
frame's yellow outline 40
highlights, adjusting 94
horizontal vs vertical see orientation of
importing from folder 74
labeling 10, 26
landscape-oriented 6
magnifying view of 5, 42, 46, 47
number in each album 27
organizing 1–30
orientation of 41, 108–113, 112, 115, 117, 119, 120, 122, 126, 128, 133, 137
overlapping 58
panning 54–55, 85, 90–91
panorama, creating 54
placing 40–41, 52–53, 63
rating 11
rearranging on page 52–53
recovering from trash 26
removing from album 13
removing from book 59
restoring to Library 9
reverting to original 68, 103, 105
reviewing 7
rotating 6
saturation, adjust 95
searching for 19–21
selecting with smart album 32–33
sharpness, adjusting 95
sorting 22

straightening 95
temperature, adjusting 95
tint, adjusting 95
titles, adding 10
viewing information 26
viewing more 24
photo books
  adding photos from other album or film roll 62
  autoflowing photos in 60–61
  choosing photos for 32–33
  cost 36
  cover, creating 40–41
  creating 31–72
  cropping photos for 113, 124, 131, 138, 139
  editing text 43, 68, 140
  fixing red eye 46–47
  frames 38
  introduction page 45
  navigating in 44
  ordering 66–67
    tips 72
  organizing files 39
  overlapping photos in 58
  page design, changing 50–51, 56–57, 61, 63
  page type, changing 45, 63
  panorama, create 54–55
  PDF file 72
  placing photos 40–41, 45, 52–53, 63
  rearranging photos 52–53
  removing pages 65
    and photo browser 71
  removing photos from 59, 70
  reordering pages 64, 71
  resolution of 72
  themes 68, 107–140

photo book themes 107–140
  Baby Boy and Baby Girl
    124–125
  Catalog 136–137
  choosing 36–37
  Classic 126–127
  Collage 130–131
  Contemporary 118–119
  Crayon 122–123
  Folio 120–121
  Picture Book 108–113
  Portfolio 132–133
  Story Book 128–129
  Travel 114–115
  Watercolor 116–117
  Year Book 134–135
photo browser
  and Autoflow 61, 70
  and changing page type 68
  in Book mode 38
  in Slideshow mode 77
  newly added photos in 62
  reducing and enlarging 77
  removing pages with 71
  removing photos from 70
  reordering pages 64
photo frames 38. See frames,
    photo
placing photos 45, 52–53, 63
  on cover 40–41
Play button
  for reviewing images 7
  for slideshows 77
Portfolio book theme 132–133
Preferences command 16
Preview button 84, 85, 93
proportion. See format,
    slideshow and 4: 3 proportion
purple keywords 29
Push transition 90–91

Q

QuickTime movies of slideshows
  101

R

ratings
  applying 11, 25, 27
  choosing by 30
  searching by 26
  sorting by 30
  tips 27
  viewing 26
rearranging photos
  and page design 69
  in books 52–53
  in slideshows 75, 82
Red-Eye tool 47
reducing the view 75
red eye, fixing 46–47
red keywords 29
red outlined number 75
Remove Page command 65
Remove Photo command 59
removing pages 65
  and photo browser 71
removing photos
  from albums 13
  from book 59, 70
  from Library 8
  permanently 9
reordering pages 64
  individual pages 71
Repeat music during slideshow
    option 106
resolution of photo book 72
Restore to Photo Library
    command 9, 26
Revert to Original command 68,
    103, 105
reviewing photos 7
  slideshow control tips 25
Roll Name field 2
  importing photos from disk 3
Rotate button 6
Rotate Clockwise command 24
Rotate Counter Clockwise
    command 24
rotating photos 6
  changing default direction
    25
  keyboard shortcuts for
    24–25

S

saturation, adjusting 95
scanned photos, importing 23
searching 19–21
  by date 20
    tips 29
  by keyword 19
    tips 29
  by text 21
    tips 30
Search box 21
selection shortcuts 25
Send Photo to Back command
  69
Send to iDVD command 106
Sepia effect 104
settings
  for books 140
  for slideshows 78–79
Settings box 140
Settings button, for photo books
  68
sharpness, adjusting 95
Show Fonts command 43
Show my ratings option 102–
  103
Show photo count for albums
  command 27
Show slideshow controls option
  102
Show titles option 102–103
size of photo 26. See
    also enlarging photos and
    magnifying the view
size of photo book 36
slideshows 73–106
  adding motion to photos
    86–87
  adding photos from other
    albums 92
  adjusting default settings
    78–79
  arranging photos in 75, 82,
    92
  centering photos 85
  controls for 106
  creating 76–77

index

cropping photos for 80–81, 88–89, 103
displaying photos in black and white 83
duplicating photos 82
duration of slide, adjusting 84
enlarging photos 85
exporting 101
format 79, 80–81, 103
keyboard shortcuts 25
music, adding 98–99
output format. See format
overview 77
panning from one half to another 88–91
pausing 106
photo browser 77
playing 100
Play button 77
Preview button 77
QuickTime movie versions 101
sharing 101
transitions, choosing 84
transition direction, changing 96–97
transition speed, adjusting 84
Slideshow Format menu 79
Slideshow mode 76–77
smart albums
and sorting 34
creating 32–33
sorting photos 22
by film rolls 4
in slideshow 75
manually 34–35
Source list
albums in 12–13
and book icon 38
camera in 2
spacebar, for pausing slideshow 106
special page designs 52
speed of transition
adjusting 84
setting default 78

spreads
adding to book 71
creating panorama across 54
reordering 64
viewing 49
square frames 129, 130–131, 137, 140
stars. See ratings
Start/End toggle 86–87, 90–91
Story Book book theme 128–129
straightness, adjusting 95

T

temperature, adjusting 95
text
automatic captions 121, 133, 136, 138, 139, 140
editing 43, 138–139
searching by 21
yellow warning triangle 68
tint, adjusting 95
titles
adding to photos 10
origin of 26
sorting photos by 30
viewing 10
transition
choosing 84, 90–91, 93
setting default 78
transition direction
changing 90–91, 96–97, 105
setting default 78
Transition menu 93
Trash
emptying 9, 26
icon 9
move photos to 8
recovering photos from 9, 26
Travel book theme 114–115. See also Chapter 2
colored blank pages 138
triangles
next to film rolls 4
next to folders 15
yellow warning 68, 69, 72
two-page spreads. See spreads

V

vertical black bar, and sorting manually 35, 75
vertical photos. See orientation of photos
viewing. See also magnifying the view
film rolls 4
keywords 18
photos 5
spreads 49
View controls 49

W

Watercolor book theme 116–117
web site, for this book xiii
widescreen format
for slideshows 102
in Contemporary book 118
Wipe transition 78
changing direction of 96–97

Y

Year Book book theme 134–135
yellow outline, of photo frames 40, 53, 57
yellow warning triangles 68, 69
and ordering book 72

Z

zoom controls. See magnifying the view and enlarging photos